Pearl,

Thanks for your prayers
&

Keep looking up

Ron Col 3; 1, 2

Relational Evangelism
for Today

Ron Bowen

xulon
PRESS

Relational Evangelism for Today
by Ron Bowen

Printed in the United States of America

ISBN 9781625098498

Unless otherwise indicated, Bible quotations are taken from The New American Standard Version of the Bible. Copyright © 1995 by The Lockman Foundation.

www.xulonpress.com

Contents

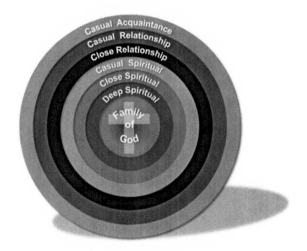

Introduction

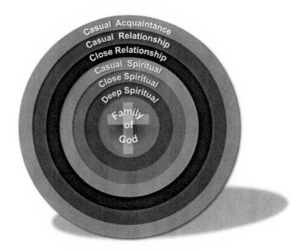

*I*t was time to downsize. The housing market was good, so we decided to sell our large home on a wooded acre lot and move to a smaller home in a planned community. So we looked, and God clearly directed us to a 55+ golf community, and as He did He placed our neighbors on our hearts.

Our community is very active, and golf is only one aspect. Our community also has summer concerts in our open-air amphitheater. While enjoying one of those concerts, I looked over our neighbors of whom we knew only a few at the time, and God simply impressed on me that this mission field was my responsibility. He clearly showed me that no matter where our neighbors were spiritually, I needed to point them to Christ. As David Jeremiah said, "The greatest untapped harvest fields in modern America are our neighborhoods."

At that time I was building some relationships and having some spiritual conversations with a few folks, but it was progressing slowly. God then supplied us with some great resources. A Christian couple, Jamie and Pam Jackson, whom we knew slightly, moved into the neighborhood. They were a great source of encouragement and have since become good friends. Also God provided a Christian golf pro, Hunter Wood, for support. Through both Jamie and Hunter we managed to start a pre-golf Bible study on Mondays before our men's golf league. The 15-minute devotional grew into a

Tuesday night Bible study, and God has been working in a mighty way since.

One of the first relationship opportunities that God brought to me was Malcolm. I met Malcolm playing golf on our regular men's golf day, Monday, and on our interclub team that plays on Thursdays. Malcolm wasn't our lowest handicap golfer, but he was certainly our most competitive. So through golf I developed a casual relationship with Malcolm. For the first three years I was the captain of the interclub team, and Malcolm played regularly on the team. On one hot summer day we played an away match, and everything seemed to go fine. Nobody appeared to be hurt by the heat, but on the following morning after the match Malcolm woke up and found that he couldn't see. From his perspective he was completely blind. He later found that that one eye was damaged, and the sight from his good eye had been impacted, but at the beginning he couldn't see at all. Since I was the captain, I felt I had the liberty to visit Malcolm and ask others on the team to pray for him.

Through this tragedy our casual relationship became closer. Malcolm's damaged eye eventually was healed over a period of about six months, and after that time he was my most regular attendee at the pre-golf Bible study. Malcolm had been raised in a religious cult environment as a child and had been damaged by religion. Over the time of his attending the pre-golf Bible study and the Tuesday night Bible study, we had many spiritual conversations. The discussions were at first casual but eventually became very deep, as he would constantly say, "I just can't believe this stuff." But he would continue to attend and actually started to come to our church, McLean Bible Church, on a regular basis. God in His wisdom moved Malcolm's nephew, Patrick, into our neighborhood. Patrick, a believer, started coming to our Tuesday night Bible studies and was a great encouragement to his uncle. Shortly after Patrick started attending, he encouraged Malcolm to accept Christ as his personal Savior. Malcolm has since moved to Florida and is tearing up the senior golfers down there. Malcolm has been a great friend, and he is now a brother in Christ. It is to Malcolm Caponiti that I dedicate this book.

My hope and prayer is that this book will encourage you to build relationships in your community, workplace, or family, and through those relationships point people to Christ.

Chapter 1

Remember

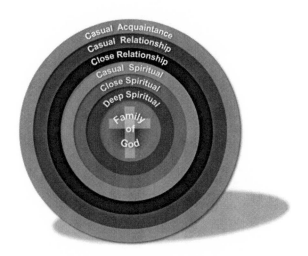

*I*f you have been a Christian for any length of time, you have been exposed to various evangelistic strategies. You feel as if you have heard it all and you may be asking yourself an important question: Why would I need to read another book on evangelism? My question to you is this: How is your current evangelistic strategy working? Have the evangelistic books you have read or witnessing classes you have taken improved your personal evangelism? Has the Bible changed? Has God's great plan of salvation changed? *Absolutely not!* However, your evangelistic mindset may need to change in order for you to be a more successful "fisher of men."

We all desire to be evangelistic. As believers, we want to be obedient to Christ's "Great Commission", but we rarely engage in spiritual conversations with unbelievers. When we do, the conversations tend to be forced and they usually go something like this:

You're in your carpool riding to work and some-body brings up the subject about people now calling Christmas trees holiday trees. That's when you jump in and say, "We are taking Christ out of Christmas," and in response to your comments, no one says a word – dead silence. However, you feel like you have taken care of your evangelistic duty for another year. . . *great.*

Is that it? Should you do more? If so, can you be successful at it, or is evangelism just for pastors? What did God say in II Timothy 4:5? "But you, be sober in all things, endure hardship, do the work of an evangelist, fulfill your ministry." Is your comment in the carpool doing the work of an evangelist, or should there be more to it than that? If so, why is it so hard and why are your attempts at evangelism rarely well received?

If the Bible hasn't changed and God's plan of salvation hasn't changed, what has changed and why is effective evangelism so difficult to accomplish today? Even more importantly, how can we become more effective evangelists in today's culture?

Answering those questions is the focus of this book.

However, before we begin to answer those questions, please take a minute and think about some of the people God used in your life to lead you to knowing Him. Perhaps they were friends, relatives, or coworkers. Maybe they were fellow soldiers or college students. As you remember some of the interactions you had with them, you also may recall how you reacted to their witness. Perhaps you initially rejected the concept of God and Christ. However, in His plan of salvation for you, God continued to bring people across your path to bear witness and play a role in your decision to accept Christ as your personal Savior.

Now remember. . .

In retrospect, do you think of these people with antagonistic or loving thoughts? They were a part of the process God used and as a result your life was changed forever. You will never be the same; you are a new creature. Of course your thoughts are filled with love and gratitude toward those special people. In the same way, you can influence people and move them toward God, and after they have put their faith in Christ they will remember you in a positive way. How great is that! I would like to tell you about a few people in my life whom God used to bring me to Him. First, is my wife Carol of 49 years. Carol was raised in a Christian home by a single parent, her mother. When we met at the age of 16, Carol was a committed Christian, and I was not a believer. She was a great encouragement to me. Actually, some of our dates would be to attend services and events at her church. It was at one of those events that I gave my life to Christ.

Another person who influenced my life was my maternal grandmother, Alma Catt. She taught me to pray at an early age and had a life committed to God through some very difficult times. Just before she went to be with the Lord, her pastor asked her what the secret to life was. She quickly responded "keep looking up." This is reflected in Colossians 3:1, 2: "Therefore if you have been raised up with Christ, keep seeking the things above, where Christ is, seated at the right hand of God. Set your mind on the things above, not on the things that on the earth." So in memory to her, I put "LOOK UP" on my license plate. When people ask what it means, I simply say that it is the secret to life, and obviously, I get a wide variety of responses.

Finally, there are two more people who influenced my decision for Christ, both friends of mine in high school. The first is Bob Varnum, who was a great friend. Bob and I played basketball and spent a lot of time hanging out together. Bob wanted to go into the Marines, and then after his military service become a pastor. I respected him for his desires. However, tragically in our senior year of high school a train hit Bob's car, and his life was taken. Needless to say I was shocked that God would allow his life to be taken when he had such high spiritual goals. I didn't understand why he had to die and others who don't even recognize that God exists were still allowed to live. Bob was a close friend and even today, some fifty years later, I can still hear his voice say "old buddy" as he would call out in his charismatic style. I look forward to seeing him again. My other friend was my best buddy and best man at my wedding, Pressley Campbell. I simply say that through Press, I found new life in Christ and took his girlfriend (my wife Carol): the two greatest things in my life!

My first witnessing moment came when I was motivated enough to ask my mother about her spiritual condition at her hospital bedside. Mom contracted ovarian cancer at the age of 47 and died before her 49th birthday. She would ask me to pray, which was the first time I prayed in public; and during one of those visits, I got up enough nerve to ask her about her spiritual condition. It took a lot at that time in my life to initiate a spiritual conversation, and that conversation was the first. I will also look forward to seeing her again as it has been 39 years since we talked. Needless to say, I was quite nervous and fearful; however, I was so motivated by my love for my mother that I overcame my fears and did the work of an evangelist.

In the next chapter we will look at some of the fears that stop or deter us from initiating spiritual conversations and explore some effective ways that we can be obedient to reaching out to others for Christ.

Small group discussion or personal reflection questions

(See possible small group format at the end of the book)

1. Who did God use to bring you to faith in Christ?

   • Write him or her a note or call this week to say "Thank you!"

2. How is your current evangelistic strategy working?

3. If you can remember, tell about your first attempt at evangelism.

   • If you can't remember your first, tell about a past attempt.

4. Tell about a recent attempt of having a spiritual conversation with a possible unbeliever.

Chapter 2

Why Don't We Evangelize?

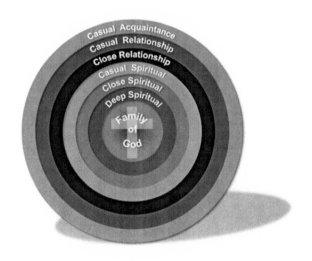

Casual Acquaintance
Casual Relationship
Close Relationship
Casual Spiritual
Close Spiritual
Deep Spiritual
Family of God

*T*here can be several obstacles to our having a spiritual conversation with anyone. Probably the first and foremost one is what we believe an evangelist should look like.

Wrong Perception of Evangelists

We often think that a person who is evangelistic must be pushy, aggressive, and arrogant in order to force people to make a decision for Christ. Or we think evangelists are super Christians with extreme charisma who are always full of great joy. The truth is that God can use you as an evangelist exactly where you are spiritually and how you interact personally. So once we get past the idea of needing to change ourselves, we can still have other fears that slow us down.

Fear
. . . of words

I know my initial fear was saying the wrong thing. I actually thought that I was responsible for the salvation of that person, and if I didn't do it right, he or she would be lost forever. How arrogant of me to think that I had any power or authority that could thwart God's plan of salvation for anyone. In fact, He just gives us the privilege to be a part of the process not determine the outcome; only Christ can affect the result. Once I had that notion straight in my mind, God used me to lead my first person to salvation.

At that time, Carol and I were attending a small church that God was using in a mighty way, and many were coming to a personal faith in Christ. It was an exciting time! One Sunday we had a small social in the basement of the church after the evening service. As I started to go downstairs, I noticed a car parked with its motor running at the entrance to the church. I approached the driver and asked if I could help him in any way. He informed me that his wife had gone to church earlier, and he was there to pick her up. I told him about the social and offered to take him downstairs to find his wife since I didn't know her. He left the car running, and we proceeded downstairs. While we were going down one set of stairs his wife was coming up the other. She then saw their car running and for some reason got in and drove home. Needless to say, her husband was a bit surprised when we came back upstairs to find the car no longer there. Without much thought, I offered to take him home.

After getting into my car, I felt led to ask him about his faith and share the gospel message. While still in the church's parking lot we proceeded to discuss the gospel, and he prayed to trust Christ as his Savior. That was my first, and what a thrill it was! He later told me the reason he listened was that I offered to take him home without asking where he lived. Truly God was at work.

. . . of questions

Another fear is that we won't know the answers to their questions. My fear of not being able to answer the difficult questions did create a hesitation in trying to have a spiritual conversation with people. At that time I didn't have any training in evangelism nor had I taken any Bible classes. I didn't know what I didn't know, and it was very inhibiting until I attended a men's breakfast at which the guest speaker was a pastor from a neighboring church. He was the senior pastor of a fairly large congregation at that time. He proceeded to give us encouragement in the area of evangelism and related his own personal fears.

One of those fears was also not being able to answer their questions. He was a senior pastor and a Bible college graduate with much personal Bible study under his belt and had the same fear. Just hearing him share the same fear I had been struggling with removed the pressure I felt by stating that we don't have to know all the answers. We can simply say, I DON'T KNOW. As the old cliché (and Biblical truth) goes, honesty is the best policy. This was again another reminder to me that another person's salvation is not in my hands. If I don't know an answer, I can just simply say, "I don't know." Sounds simple enough, but it was a great relief to me. We don't have to know all of the answers to their questions for God to use us.

. . . of rejection

Probably the strongest fear of all is the fear of being rejected. To be looked at like we are aliens from another planet or that we are viewed as being completely out of touch with reality can be damaging to our egos and cause us to go back into our shells and never pop our heads out again. But we must come to understand that they are not rejecting us; they are rejecting God. In Luke 10:16, Christ says, "The one who listens to you listens to Me, and the one who rejects you rejects Me." We are simply God's messengers, and they are really rejecting Him. How sad is that? They are rejecting the God who can bring them true joy and save them from eternal punishment.

We need to take ourselves out of the picture and not take the rejection of our message personally. Their battle is with God, and our witness could still be just one step in their conversion process. Maybe at some point later in life he or she will make a decision for Christ. Later in the book we will learn that as we build relationships with people, the likelihood of being rejected goes down dramatically. They might not be receptive to the message, but they won't get ugly about it because of our relationship with them.

. . . of failure

In going through the book with our McLean Bible Church small group another fear was discussed, the fear of failure. This is similar to the other fears mentioned but is slightly different. This is the case in which we do everything right, and we answer their questions, but they still don't respond. In this case we feel that we have failed. Although we should try to be careful in building relationships and having spiritual conversations, which we will discuss later in the book, the outcome or result is <u>totally</u> with the Lord. Proverbs 21:31 states "The horse is prepared for battle but victory belongs to the Lord." We should prepare and do the best we can but our performance <u>does not</u> determine the outcome.

Often it seems like the times when I struggle with leading a Bible study, or teaching a class, or having a spiritual conversation, people will tell me later how God used it in their lives. Our success is not with the outcome but is in having that spiritual conversation that God can use. So if we are afraid of failure we are thinking incorrectly just as I was with the fear of saying the wrong thing. We are thinking that our words or performance will save them and not the Holy Spirit. So leave the results with God, that's where the victory belongs.

As we face our fears the most important thing to remember is that love overcomes fear. I John 4:18a tells us, "There is no fear in love; but perfect love casts out fear." Just as a mother will go into a burning house to get her child, so our love for those who are headed for eternal separation from God should help us to overcome our fears. Also to help us to increase our love for others is to remember the One who loves us. I John 4:19 states that we love because He first loved us.

Lack of Experience

We may have faced obstacles, and because of those obstacles we lack experience. I can honestly say that the more you have spiritual conversations with people, the easier those conversations will be; but it will always be a spiritual battleground. The enemy will always attempt to sidetrack us. So the only way to gain experience is just to have spiritual conversations with a proper loving approach that will not be offensive to those you are trying to reach.

Not Using the Proper Technique

Not knowing or using the best evangelistic technique for our time and culture may be another reason why we are not inclined to witness. Failure to recognize that technique can be important and can impact our effectiveness.

Several past evangelistic techniques were very successful because they fit the culture at that time. Evangelism Explosion (EE) started at Coral Ridge Presbyterian Church in Florida and was extremely successful. The whole approach was based on the premise that most people believed in heaven, and that you got there by being good - God would put your works on a scale, and if your good works outweighed your bad works, you got in- which, according to the

Bible, is false. On one occasion I was leading an EE team, and we visited the home of a family who had just visited our church for the first time on the previous Sunday. The family was out for the evening, but the grandmother, an 81-year-old woman, was home by herself. At first she was skeptical, but after some discussion, she accepted Christ as her Lord and Savior. The experience was very emotional for her and the tears flowed freely because she had been carrying the guilt of her husband's suicide for several years. That was a very rewarding visit as she went to be with the Lord about six months later. That was clearly a divine appointment.

We also did "cold turkey" door-to-door evangelism. For a few years Carol and I knocked on doors together. We worked well together as a team. She would break the ice, and I would present the gospel. On one occasion we were still knocking on doors after dark. One particular townhouse had a rear entrance with no outside lights. As we went around to the back in the dark, we had to feel our way on the sidewalk with our feet. We then approached the door and knocked, the door opened, and we were very surprised to see a dog at the door, standing on all fours and looking Carol straight in the eye. It was the biggest dog we had ever seen. We thought we were going to be eaten alive. But the woman who opened the door was very gracious and invited us into her home where Carol proceeded to keep the dog under control while I presented the gospel. We had a long visit and she was very receptive but she did not receive Christ that night. Maybe we were just planting a seed that someone else would get to water and be able to harvest.

During this time I would also hand out tracts (pamphlets that presented the gospel) everywhere I went. I usually got gas on my way to work and stopped often at the same gas station. At this station and at this time you pumped your own gas, but the attendant would come out to collect the money when you finished. Since I frequented this specific station often, I had given the attendant several tracts, and on one particular day as I was pulling into the pumps I decided that I didn't want to give him another. So I threw up a quick prayer to God saying if there were no other cars getting gas at the same time, I would verbally share the gospel with him rather than just give him a tract. So, much to my dismay, when I pulled in, all of the other cars pulled out, so now I had to go through with it. The attendant came out while I was still pumping gas, and I asked him if he would he like to receive Christ as his personal savior. I was floored when he said, "Yes"! So right there between the pumps he prayed to accept Christ. I later gave him some follow-up materials, and he got involved in a church where he lived.

That was then — This is Now!

A fairly recent Barna survey (2007) revealed a changing atmosphere in our culture.

- In the mid-nineties the vast majority of Americans outside of the Christian faith felt favorably toward Christians role in society
- Today 91% of American Evangelicals believe that Americans are becoming more hostile and negative toward Christianity
- Currently only 16% of 16-29 year old non-Christians express a favorable view toward Christians in general and only 3% express a favorable view toward evangelical Christians
- Non-Christians view Christians as judgmental (87%), hypocritical (85%), and old fashioned (78%)

The most disturbing thing about this data is that these perceptions of non-Christians toward Christians are rooted in specific stories of interactions with Christians. The Core

Value #4 at McLean Bible Church is that "Ministry and evangelism must be carried out in a relevant way." So how do we do that in a culture that is anti-Christian? How do we have successful spiritual conversations with people and not just say "we need to keep Christ in Christmas." Today we must be **Relational Evangelists.** Relationship building can simply be a conversation on an airplane or developing an ongoing friendship with a neighbor. But the key is that in most evangelistic encounters today we must develop a relationship first in order to "earn" the privilege of impacting people spiritually.

An example of how our culture has become less receptive to evangelism techniques of the past is an experience a good friend of ours, Jamie Winship, had at a tollbooth a few years ago. As he passed through the tollbooth, he did what he always did and handed a tract to the tollbooth attendant. As he was driving away the attendant hollered at him to come back. He then proceeded to tell Jamie that he had no right to shove a tract at him; he didn't know him or anything about him. At that point Jamie realized that he needed to reevaluate and change his evangelism style. Instead of forcing the gospel down people's throats, he would need to build a relationship with them first. Since then, Jamie has adopted this relationship-based approach to witnessing.

Peter Frey presently a seminary student said, "I dare say the day of door to door evangelism is over, and the day of next-door evangelism is here." I agree! So in the next chapter we will explore **Relational Evangelism.**

Small group discussion or personal reflection questions

1. What is your perception of an evangelist?

2. What are the four fears discussed in the chapter?

   - Which of the fears mentioned is your strongest?

   - Do you have other fears not mentioned?

3. Do you have any past training in evangelism?

4. What are some cultural changes you have seen in your lifetime that would affect your evangelism strategy?

Chapter 3

What is Relational Evangelism?

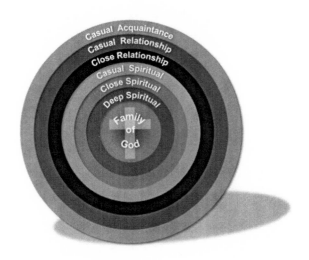

*W*e live at a time when strong relationships are not normal. We don't have those types of relationships in which we actually care about another person. . . you know, when you are willing to get up at 3:00am and help if needed. This trend is due in part to the breakup of the family unit. It is common knowledge that approximately 50% of all marriages end up in divorce, and many of those families have children who are impacted for life. Those children are typically fearful of risking relationships that may fail and cause pain. Also, traditional marriage itself is in decline. People are afraid to make permanent and lasting commitments.

Today close relationships are limited or non-existent. This lack of close personal relationships is one of the reasons for the explosion of social networking. God has created us to need human contact by having relationships with other people – to be in a community. Those who don't have deep and significant relationships will attempt to fill that void by forming many virtual relationships. Consequently, social networking is used to fill the relationship void.

Another aspect of this relationship void is that Christians are becoming more and more isolated from unbelievers. We first see this in the form of differing political views, wherein the values of the major political parties are more divided than ever on key issues such as abortion, marriage, and religious freedom. Secondly, some believers are becoming isolated in the work place. They work at a church, a para-church organization, a Christian business, or at home. Retired Christians no longer have any work contacts. Lastly, Christians are certainly becoming more isolated socially, especially in our neighborhoods. How many of your neighbors do you know by name and occupation?

Max Lucado said in his book *Out Live Your Life,* "Our society is set up for isolation. We wear our earbuds when we exercise. We communicate via e-mail and text messages. We enter and exit our houses with gates and garage-door openers. Our mantra: I leave you alone. You leave me alone. Yet God wants his people to be an exception."

A Barna 2008 survey found that:

- Atheists and agnostics were more likely to cite their workplace as their top social network.
- Christians in general were evenly divided with 1/5th identifying work, 1/5th identifying their church, and 1/5th listing their friends as their primary social network.
- 74% of all evangelicals said their church was their social network

From this summary we can see that only 20% of nominal Christians or Christians in general, claim their church as their primary social network. But 74% of more committed Christians claim the church. So, as we become more committed in our faith, we actually become more isolated from unbelievers. Therefore, if we are to reach out to those who need to hear the good news of the Gospel, we must be proactive in developing relationships with them.

Many of our churches have not yet acknowledged the reality of believers being isolated from unbelievers. However, some churches have developed evangelistic strategies like "invest and invite." In this program we are to invest intentionally in people's lives then invite them to church. The strategy is basically sound except that all of our present focus tends to be on the inviting part. Many of our churches have experienced success at becoming "seeker friendly" wanting unbelievers to feel welcome and not be distracted by traditional religious formalities. This is basically a good idea as long as the Biblical message God has given us is not diluted.

The inviting part is working. Actually a Lifeway Research survey stated that 82% of unchurched adults would consider coming to church if a friend invited them. Maybe 25% would actually come. The key here is FRIEND. If they consider you to be a friend, one in four would probably come to a church related activity if you invited them. The problem is that we do not have many unchurched friends. That's where the strategy is lacking. It doesn't focus on the investing part. We need to be investing in people's lives to BECOME their FRIENDS.

Investing takes significant time and resources if we want to make an impact in people's lives. Mark Mittleburg in his book, *Becoming a Contagious Christian* said that we must barbecue first before we invite. In other words, we must build a relationship with them before we invite them to a church related activity. Actually, it should be a lot more than barbecue, but that's the idea.

This strategy is not new to successful missionaries, as they have been doing this for years. They would risk their lives to develop relationships with the people they are trying to reach. One of many great missionary couples is Don and Carol Richardson. In Don's book *Peace Child* he explains how they risked their lives and the lives of their children to live among cannibals. They built their home and lived with them for years to develop relationships in order to have the privilege to share the greatest news in the entire world.

The natives had a reputation of building relationships in order for their enemies to let down their guard just enough so that they could kill them and devour their flesh. So you could imagine how they viewed Don and Carol. The natives probably thought that Don and Carol were building relationships with them for the same purpose. The Richardsons risked it all, and their reward was great because many natives became Christians and abandoned their previous lifestyle to embrace Christ. Our risk at attempting to build relationships with unbelievers is far less devastating. All we have to risk is our time, money, and maybe some of our reputation.

So what is Relational Evangelism?

All of our relationships are at different levels. The key is that relationships are progressive: as we get closer to someone, the opportunities for effective spiritual conversations increase in number and depth. So we must recognize that the relationship model has a target: to bring people into the family of God. The concentric rings in the figure below represent the levels of interpersonal relationship between the believer and the unbeliever, and as we approach the center, we reach the target.

Relational Evangelism

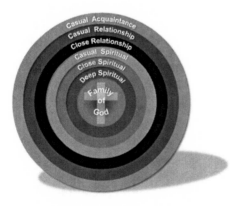

1. Casual Acquaintance
2. Casual Relationship
3. Close Relationship
4. Casual Spiritual Relationship
5. Close Spiritual Relationship
6. Deep Spiritual Relationship
7. Family of God Relationship

1 - 3 Secular Relationships
4 - 6 Spiritual Relationships

Secular Circles

In this relationship model the three outer circles represent three secular relationship levels. These are relationships that focus on getting to learn general information about the person as the precursor to discovering the person's spiritual condition. No spiritual conversations take place at these levels. The outer circle is defined as a Casual Acquaintance. This is someone who lives in the same community, shops at the same grocery store, or works in the same building. We recognize those folks, but we really don't know anything about them.

The next inner secular circle is defined as a Casual Relationship. These are people we actually know. We know their names and maybe something about their family, but that's about it. In today's environment it could be a next door neighbor. We see them come and go but don't know much about them. The final secular relationship is defined as a Close Relationship. At this point we still have not had a spiritual conversation with them, but we know where they work, what they enjoy (golf?), and something about their family. Perhaps we had them over for a barbecue or went out with them in a neighborhood dine out group. We have been involved with them in some smaller group activity, and through that activity we are getting to know them better. Perhaps we work in the same department, and we have completed a project together. But all these are still secular relationships, and we desire to move closer in order to have a spiritual conversation with them.

Spiritual Circles

The next three circles represent spiritual relationships. These are relationships where we are having some form of spiritual conversation with them. The outermost spiritual relationship is defined as a Casual Spiritual Relationship. This is a relationship in which we break the ice, spiritually. We have made the transition from the weather to perhaps where they go to church or ask whether they believe in a divine creator. So we have started, but it's early.

The second inner spiritual circle is defined as Close Spiritual Relationship. At this point, we are still getting spiritual information about them. By now we know their church background and church attendance habits. We know some of their childhood stories and such information as why they do or don't attend a church, and about how they were raised. We have invited them to church related activities, and although they have come to some, we are still not sure of their spiritual condition. The final spiritual circle is defined as Deep Spiritual Relationship. At this stage spiritual conversations are commonplace. We know where they are spiritually, and we are sharing the gospel with them in an ongoing manner when we have opportunity.

Family of God Circle

We see them moving closer to God and view it as just a matter of time until they take that step of faith. The final circle is defined as the Family of God Circle. They have taken the step to believe in Christ and now your relationship with them is changed forever. This is our bull's eye that keeps us on track throughout all of the other relationship circles or levels.

Not every relationship will start at the outer most circle and end with them accepting Christ. Some will start out there but get stalled or stop within one of the circles. Some will quickly go to the spiritually relationship level, but others will take a long time.

I had developed a relationship with a fellow golfer and had attempted to start a spiritual conversation with him. His reaction to my attempt was somewhat hostile, and clearly he did not want to go down that path. So over time I attempted to go to the next level, and again he would be hostile to the point that on one occasion I had to apologize for attempting to go farther. It has to be God that allows it to go farther, and I needed to be patient. But because of our relationship, the avenue is still there if he has a change of heart.

We can have many relationships at a time that are likely to be at different levels. In all cases it's important that we prayerfully seek God's help to move them move closer to Him. We will not always get the privilege to reap what we sow, but also we might be able to reap what others have sown. God usually works in several ways through several different people. John 4:37b - 38 says, "One sows and another reaps. I sent you to reap that for which you have not labored; others have labored and you have entered into their labor."

That's the process we will discuss in the remaining chapters. The important thing to remember is that we must be **proactive** in establishing and cultivating relationships with unbelievers.

Small group discussion or personal reflection questions

1. List the seven levels in the relationship circle model.

- Secular

- Spiritual

- Family of God

2. What is your primary social network?

3. Do you feel somewhat isolated from unbelievers? What are the causes of that isolation?

4. Discuss some of your present relationships with possible unbelievers and state where they are on the relationship level scale.

Chapter 4

"Let's Go Fishing!"
Building Casual Relationships

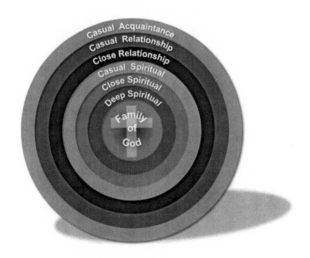

Get out there!

*T*he first and most important step in building any relation-ship is to meet them where they are. Mark 1:17 states, and Jesus said to them "Follow me and I will make you become fishers of men." A successful fisherman knows how to find the fish. He knows where they are at a specific time of the day. He knows when they go to a shady area to escape from the sun and when they go to another area to feed. So just as a fisherman finds the fish, we must be involved with unbelievers in places where they live and work. This doesn't mean we go to places or participate in   activities that God wouldn't like, but where He approves we **must** go.

Getting out there is especially hard for pastors and church staffers, as it was for me when I was on staff at a church. Your entire world is filled with believers, so you have to be especially diligent in pursuing activities in which you can build relationships with unbelievers. Also the relationship building process takes time, and we must be patient. It's just like reeling in a big fish; we need to be willing to spend the time, in the heat of the day, when we would rather be sit-ting in the shade, and slowly reel them in. I can't remember the quote exactly, but it was said that it takes a significant number of relationship building hours to bring someone to

Christ. So it could take a long time, and again we must be patient. Our pastor Lon Solomon said, "Don't give up on them; we give up on them too soon."

Get Involved!

As we become involved in non-church activities and organizations (secular groups) try to seek out those activities at which you can excel. Several years ago I was listening to a missionary speaker, Ivan Shoen, who spent several years living with a native group in South America. After seeing several of the natives become Christians he asked one of the men, "Why did you become a Christian?" And to Ivan's surprise the man didn't say it was your integrity, Bible knowledge, or love of God - even though these are vitally important. He said he became a Christian because Ivan knew a lot about gasoline engines. This statement bothered me for several years because I couldn't understand how a person's knowledge about gasoline engines could influence someone to consider Christianity. But I think it's as simple as that people will listen to what you might say about spiritual things if they respect you for something else. So in the same manner, if you can, get plugged into community activities at which you can excel, gain the respect of others, and develop relationships.

We presently live in a golf community, and I love to golf. Sports have always been a part of my life, and golf is a sport. ☺ I was the captain of our interclub team for three years and president of our men's golf association for two years. So, through the activity of golf, I could build relationships. Later in the book I will explain how I was able to integrate spiritual opportunities into my golfing activities.

My wife Carol spent most of her life singing in church groups and choirs, but she had never been involved in a community singing group. So when our community started a chorale, it was a great opportunity for her. She got plugged in and has developed many relationships through singing and performing. Other activities we have done in our community were, dining out groups, lunch groups, neighborhood socials, racket ball, exercise classes, and the like. I think you get the idea. In the past I have played a lot of softball, and God used it in the life of a guy who would become a lifelong friend.

He tells the story that the first time we met, he was pitching for the team I was playing against. I was playing for a church team, and as I approached the plate, he proceeded to size me up. I guess I looked pretty wimpy with the bat resting on my shoulder as he pitched the ball. His thought was that Christians were weak, and I fit that look until the bat met the ball, and his opinion changed. He later became a Christian, and we played together for many years, only then on the same team.

Seek out activities that you can excel at, but if you can't, at least seek out non-church activities. Joe Aldrich in his book *Life Style Evangelism* said that his neighbors were tennis players, so he became a tennis player, and two neighbors came to Christ. This is going to where the fish are. So as you develop relationships through activities, you must become involved in their lives. Paul said in I Corinthians 9:22, "To the weak I became weak that I might win the weak; I have become all things to all men, so that I may by all means save some." Paul became like those he was trying to reach without hurting his testimony. He wanted them to be comfortable around him, and he did not want to offend them in order to build relationships. Our friends Jamie and Donna Winship have spent half of their lives living overseas. They will actually change the décor of their home depending on whom they have invited over for dinner. They want the guests to feel welcome and comfortable in their home as they build relationships with them.

It's important to understand that God can use a variety of approaches and personalities to accomplish His objective in reaching people. Again, we don't have to be pushy or arrogant. We will never argue someone into the kingdom. In their book and class *Becoming a Contagious Christian*, Mark Mittleburg and Lee Strobel describe several styles that God can use in reaching people. The styles that they describe are unique to specific personality types, but they are also best used at different relationship levels. As we go through the relationship levels certain styles fit best into each specific level, and I will be referring to these styles throughout the remainder of the book. The style they call "interpersonal" is first and foremost used in building casual relationships. The characteristics of an interpersonal style as they describe are conversational, having relational warmth, and being friendship-oriented. This style is critical in the early stages of a relationship, but it also can apply to some degree at all levels. Even though this may not be our dominant style, we all must build friendships with those who are unbelievers; therefore, we must interact in a positive way with them. This is a style I needed to learn and adopt because it wasn't my natural tendency. But as we care about people, this approach will become easier.

The first step in building casual relationships is going to where they are, and this means being involved in secular group activities. Bill Hybels said we must "Walk Across the Room." So first we must be in the room, and second, we must walk to them. We must be proactive and deliberate with our time in reaching out to people. So go. . . and then be patient.

What are some non-church activities that God could use in your life to develop relationships? Maybe you could start an activity such as a monthly game night or card club. Others have started or plugged into biking and walking groups. Do you have a pet? Dog owners love to talk about their dogs while walking them. Take a watercolor class at a local community college or activity center. Volunteer in a school or hospital. Audition for a community theatre group. Feel uncomfortable going it alone? Bring a Christian friend along, but have the same goal: to make new friends. But whatever activity you get involved in get there early and leave late. The time before and after the activity is important in building relationships.

Now we can develop some relationships, but how do we get closer to them in order to have spiritual conversations?

Small group discussion or personal reflection questions

1. What two things do you need to do to meet unbelievers?

2. What are some community activities that you are involved in?

3. What are some activities in your community that you could get involved in?

   • Could you start an activity?

4. What are some on the job activities that you could do in order to build relationships?

Chapter 5

"May I Help You?"
Building Close Relationships

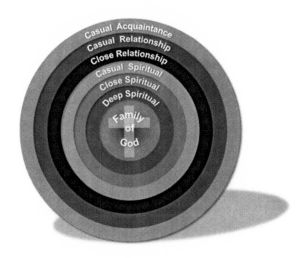

*A*t this point we have established several casual relationships, but we need to grow closer to some of them so that we can have more personal conversations in order to move from just secular to spiritual discussions. To do this we should go from group activities to one-on-one or two-on-two activities because people are more open about themselves in a smaller group. For me I would look for opportunities to golf with a smaller more regular set of guys. I actually finished my basement and put in a putting green and driving net so that I could invite others over to use. I think this was the main reason, but it has improved my putting. ☺ In her chorale group, Carol started a birthday card ministry in which she would send cards to women in the chorale or in the neighborhood. Through this simple act of kindness, she touched hearts, and the women were truly grateful.

Look For Opportunities

We must be always on the lookout for opportunities to develop closer relationships through one-on-one or small group activities. One way to do this is to recognize where God is at work and get involved. As I explained in the introduction, one opportunity came after a normal summer interclub golf match. It was especially hot that day, but everything seemingly went okay. We didn't have any cases of heat exhaustion as we were very careful. But on the following morning one of the golfers got up in the morning and couldn't see. From his perspective he was totally blind. As captain I felt the responsibility and opportunity to move closer. I immediately visited him and offered my prayers. I also asked other golfers to pray. After going to a doctor he realized that only one eye was damaged, but it affected the sight for the good eye. So by patching the bad eye he could see, and over a period of several months the damaged eye healed to the point of being almost normal. So through the damaged eye a close relationship got started and eventually led to his trusting Christ as his personal savior.

Love Them

Taking this step in going beyond a secular and casual relationship takes love and commitment. We must truly be interested in them, their struggles, their successes, and their lives. This is where we must "Love your neighbor as yourself" (Leviticus 19:18).

We live in Virginia, and the last couple of winters we have had an abundance of snow. At the time of one of these snowfalls, I was preparing a Sunday school lesson on relational evangelism, so the Great Commandment was on my heart as I was outside shoveling snow. I grew up in Western Pennsylvania, and we also lived in upstate New York for five years, so snow had been a part of our lives. Also since the winters were longer there, we were very careful in our snow shoveling techniques. I would push and throw the snow on the downwind side, always shovel to the edges to let the sun clear off the remaining snow, shovel all sidewalks, and clear off a place in front of the mailbox for the mailperson. I had completed our home area and proceeded to go to our neighbors' home. They were several years older than we were and not able to shovel.

As I started, I was cold and tired, so I attempted to cut corners where I could. They had a two car garage but only had one car so my reasoning was to only clear one side of the driveway. Also, I thought they didn't need to use their sidewalk. They could just go through the garage and down the driveway to get the mail. While shoveling God reminded me of that little verse found in Mark 12, The Great Commandment. So in my mind I questioned, "What does it really mean to love your neighbor as yourself?" So as God spoke to me in this situation, I understood that He clearly doesn't mean for me to cut corners on my neighbor's snow. I should actually shovel my neighbor's driveway and sidewalk in the same way that I would do my own. So I cleared everything to the edges, the way a true New Yorker would do.

For Carol one opportunity came through the death of a neighbor's husband. We live in a 55 and over community, so the battle of health issues is always prevalent. Carol reached out and offered food, help, conversation, and friendship. Our pastor Lon Solomon says "Always be ready to grab the opportunity when it comes up. Sooner or later a crisis will strike their lives and suddenly that door of unbelief that has been closed will swing wide open."

Use Your Financial Resources

I am a proponent of Biblical financial stewardship. I have taught several classes in Biblical finances and have been the primary financial counselor at a couple of previous churches we attended. So budgeting has been a vital part of our lives. A few years ago God impressed on me to establish an evangelism budget, a line item in our home budget that I would only use for evangelism. Jesus said in Luke 16:9, "I tell you, use worldly wealth to gain friends for yourselves, so that when it is gone, you will be welcomed into eternal dwellings." (NIV) So we should use our financial resources to win people to Christ. Therefore I established this budget item to address evangelistic opportunities when they come up. Just after I made my first deposit into my evangelism line item, God presented an opportunity to use it.

At that time we lived in a reasonably well-to-do community, and door-to-door salesman were common. On one afternoon a young man from the inner city knocked on our door to sell magazines. I normally would have refused, but since I had some money in my evangelism budget, I let him in. He had a great lead-in question to sell magazines. He simply asked to what do you attribute your success. For me this was a great lead-in to the gospel, and since I had some money set aside, I could purchase some magazines for the opportunity to give out the gospel. So I proceeded, and he was very attentive. After my presentation and commitment to buy three years of Golf Digest, I asked him the closing question. I asked him if he would like to pray and receive Christ right now.

To my surprise he agreed, and my immediate thought was that he was willing to go a long way to sell a magazine. So he prayed, and I encouraged him to get involved in an inner city church, and we parted ways. . . or so I thought. Throughout the day he proceeded through our neighborhood and came to our neighbor's home across the street after dark. He told them of our experience, and they said he should come back to my house and get some follow-up material to start his Christian walk. So after dark and late at night he came back to my door. I gave him what I had and praised God for this new found opportunity knowing that the salesman would never have returned unless his decision was sincere. God continued to use the evangelism budget over the years, and I strongly encourage you to start one today, and then sit back and watch God work.

Serve Them

As we build close relationships, the best style to use from *Becoming a Contagious Christian* is the serving style. Mark Mittleberg said, "Our message of love has much more impact when preceded by our acts of love." Removing snow, sending birthday cards, getting their mail, buying magazines, and watching their kids are acts of love that can open a door to the greatest message of love. The serving style as defined by Mark and Lee is being others-oriented, working behind the scenes, and showing patience.

We have been building close relationships by looking for opportunities where God is already at work and serving in them with a loving heart. Now we are ready to cross the threshold of secular relationships. We have gotten close through secular activities, and now we must see if our friends are open to spiritual conversations.

Small group discussion or personal reflection questions

1. What kind of service activities can you do in your community?

2. How can you use your financial resources to impact lives?

   • Are you willing to start an evangelism budget?

3. Who can you have a one-on-one or two-on-two meeting with?

   • How? When? Where?
     o Barbecue, coffee, dinner, walking

4. Is there someone in your community who is going through some sort of struggle?

   • How can you reach out to him or her?

Chapter 6

"Let's Talk about God"
Building Casual Spiritual
Relationships

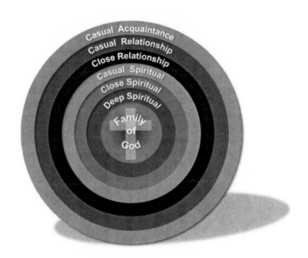

*W*e have developed a secular relationship through group and one-on-one activities, but we haven't yet had any spiritual conversations with our new friends. This is where most people get stalled. We are convinced that we can witness by our lifestyle, which is important, but in order to have a spiritual conversation, we must say something. We must take that first step and turn a natural or normal conversation into a spiritual one. Before we do this, we need some proper preparation.

This proper preparation is just in two parts, prayer and place. We must be praying for God to soften their hearts and that they would be open to discuss where they are spiritually. So develop an evangelical prayer list. Make this a list of people who need Christ and who you have a relationship with. Then pray for them daily. Always be open to add new people to the list. Pray specifically for the next step in the relationship process. If it's to start a spiritual conversation, pray for wisdom and the right words, so that they would be receptive and that they would respond positively.

The second part in preparation is to have a place. We must create a safe environment where you can find out where they are spiritually. So move to a more conversational environment by continuing the one-on-one meetings. This could be a deliberate meeting such as a breakfast or dinner, or could be as simple as driving to play golf or racquetball. They must be free to speak openly. They rarely will be open in front of others, so the one-on-one is important.

Questioning

Now that they are prayed up, and we have a place; we must be ready to start a spiritual conversation by asking a question. We need to have at least one question ready. My most used question is "Do you attend church?" or "Are you a church goer?" This is usually non-threatening and yet can give you a lot of insight to where they are spiritually, but be ready with the second question if they respond. A few responses I have received are:

- "Yes, I go regularly to _____ church." From here I see as a green light to go deeper. Some of my responses could be:
    - o Depending on the church type, I might respond with, "Do you study the Bible?" or "Have you been involved in any Bible studies in your church?"
    - o "Is this the church type in which you were raised or have you changed?"
    - o Sometimes I respond, "Since you have been involved at your church, have you come to the place where you have accepted Jesus as your personal Savior?"
- "No, I don't attend a church." From here I might respond.
    - o "Did you attend a church as a child and stop as an adult?"
    - o "Have you ever been interested in religion?"
    - o "Did you ever attend a church?"
        - ▪ "If so, what made you stop?"

o If they are open, this could lead to a discussion about evolution or intelligent design.
o If they are not open, it usually stops here, and I'll look for other opportunities in the future.

Asking about their church background is one approach. A deeper approach is to use Jamie's question, "Have you ever heard God speak?" We will discuss this in chapter 8. If you can, ask simple probing questions from which you can gain insight to where they are spiritually. But in all cases be sensitive and truthful. Colossians 4:5, 6, "Conduct yourselves with wisdom toward outsiders, making the most of the opportunity. Let your speech always be with grace, as though seasoned with salt, so that you will know how you should respond to each person." John MacArthur states: "Speak what is wholesome, fitting, kind, sensitive, purposeful, complimentary, gentile, truthful, loving, and thoughtful." Anyway, you get the idea.

Have one question ready that can jump-start a spiritual conversation, but also be ready for other more natural or bridge transitions to spiritual conversations.

Bridging

People from all over the world like to talk about their family. When we were visiting missionary friends in the jungles of Indonesia, a common question from the natives was always around family. Actually family was so important that they would change their name with the birth of a child or grandchild. So instead of Ron, my name would have been "the father of Renee" after the birth on my daughter and then changed to "the grandfather of Kayla" after the birth of my granddaughter.

I simply use family as a Christian icebreaker. I would say that our family is perfectly balanced just as you should strive for balance in the Christian life. We have a son and daughter and our son and daughter each has a son and daughter. We were on a Caribbean cruise, and at one stop we were walking from the ship to the tour busses, and a man started walking with us. I used the family Christian ice breaker, and by the time we reached the busses, I had learned most of his spiritual/religious background.

On one occasion we were out to dinner with our neighbors, and our discussion centered on medical issues and operations because our neighbor was soon to go through a major surgery and was very concerned. I simply stated that I was presently reading a book on Heaven by Randy Alcorn and that when we get to heaven we will receive a new body without the need for surgery and doctors. From this opening I was able to explain the gospel message completely.

Current events are a very popular topic especially with the unrest in the Middle East. I like to cite the example of the nation of Israel. They were scattered throughout the world around 70AD and brought back and reestablished as a nation in 1948. Typically any people group that is conquered or scattered loses its national identity in 3-4 generations or about 120 – 160 years. However, Israel was reestablished after about 1900 years. Only God could do this. After this fact I usually get the chance to discuss God's future plan which includes Israel.

Bridging to spiritual conversations can take some planning. Think of a statement or comment that would be a good transition statement for you. But also be ready to bridge from the conversation or situation at hand. While going for a walk and looking at the beauty of nature you could talk about the complexity and balance in nature that only a God could orchestrate. Maybe you are discussing an upcoming holiday like Christmas or Easter. You might simply ask how they typically celebrate it. Be creative and natural.

Bridging is important. Some Christians maintain a close relationship for several years and never find out where their friends are spiritually. Bill Hybels states that only 10% of Christians ever break the ice and have spiritual conversations with non-Christians. So we all must be a part of the 10% and take the plunge. If you have laid the relationship foundation, even a rejection at this point will not normally constitute a break in the relationship. You will probably have other opportunities in the future; look for them!

Invite to church related activities

After you have broken the ice with a spiritual conversation, a good follow-up to that would be to invite them to a church related event. As I stated in chapter 3, 25% of unchurched adults would probably come to church if a friend invited them. Sometimes when our church has a ticketed event, we simply buy some extra tickets and pray for the "friend" we should invite. On one occasion we did this for our Christmas program and invited a neighborhood couple. The guy was blown away with the brass band that performed because he used to play in a brass band. From that invitation he loved our church became a faithful attender.

By inviting a friend to a church event, you could be helping someone come back to church. A 2011 Barna survey stated that adult church attendance has dropped by 11% for women and 6% for men over the last twenty years.

As we build casual spiritual relationships the best style to use from *Becoming a Contagious Christian* would be the Invitational style. To demonstrate an invitational style you would be hospitable, relational, and persuasive.

Give out books and CDs

The previous example is inviting them to a church related event, but you could also invite them to read a book or listen to a CD. Giving books and CDs can be especially good for short-term relationships that you know are coming to a close. When we have someone over to work on the house, I like to hang around and talk to him if I am at home. From our relational talk I like to give a copy of our pastor's (Lon Solomon) testimonial CD. He had a dramatic conversion, and his testimony has impacted many lives. On one of these occasions through our relational conversation, I discovered that the worker's wife was a Christian, but he was resistant because he didn't agree with the concept of once saved, always saved. So I gave him the book *Eternal Security* by Charles Stanley.

We must be bridgers and inviters to impact lives. As we bridge and invite, we attempt to move them closer and to move from a casual spiritual relationship to a close spiritual relationship.

Small group discussion or personal reflection questions

1. What two things does the proper preparation include?

2. What is a good spiritual conversation starter question that you could use?

3. With whom does God want you to have to have a spiritual conversation?

4. To what church related activity could you invite a friend?

5. What book or CD could be your regular evangelistic gift?

6. Who can you put on your evangelistic prayer list and pray for regularly?

Chapter 7

"Got Questions?" Building Close Spiritual Relationships

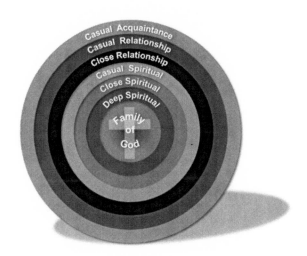

*W*e have progressed in our relationship; now we know some of their spiritual background. We understand what they believe, and we may even know what some of their objections are to the Christian faith. So this is where we start. We must begin at the point of where they are spiritually. Paul started from creation for pagans and from the Old Testament for Jews. But before we attempt to move them closer to Christ, we should discuss with them the areas in which we agree. By first having discussions on which we agree, we are making our new friends comfortable in having spiritual discussions, which makes the next step in the process easier.

I golf with a person of the Muslim faith, and he is very comfortable discussing spiritual issues with me. We first started at creation with Adam and Eve. We now discuss areas of difference, but it's not argumentative, and we maintain a good relationship.

Relational Seeker Small Groups

Continue the one-on-ones and go deeper with your spiritual conversations. But as you develop these relationships you might consider starting a Relational Seeker Small Group. This is a group Bible study around a specific activity.

It must be convenient and Bible light. We have a men's golf outing/league every Monday during the summer and get sometimes 60-70 men in our community out for golf. So I started a 15 minute pre-golf Bible study before our shotgun start. We normally start at 9:00am, so I would have the Bible study from 8:15am – 8:30am in the office of our club pro. At first no one would come, but eventually it grew to 10-12 guys.

Think about what you could do around your activity. Perhaps with a walking or biking group, you could have a small Bible study after or before you head out.

Another way to do a Relational Seeker Small Group is around a specific topic or book. This could be a one-time only meeting to discuss such things as:

- Is Jesus really God?
- Evolution vs. Intelligent Design
- Raising Daughters/Sons
- Being a good Husband/Wife

You could use a DVD or just discuss the topic and invite those you have had some spiritual conversations with. It would be good if the invitee list included some Christians that they already know and have a relationship with. Then the discussions would have perspectives from other Christians as well and not just yours. A good resource for these kinds of groups is *Seeker Small Groups* by Gary Poole.

At this point in your relationship you will get more questions, and you will have fewer answers. But that is good because witnessing will cause you to study. Paul stated in II Timothy 2:15 "Study to show thyself approved unto God, a workman that needeth not to be ashamed, rightly dividing the word of truth." (KJV)

Apologetics

But try to be ready. I Peter 3:15 states: "But sanctify Christ as Lord in your hearts, always being ready to make a defense to everyone who asks you to give an account for the hope that is in you, yet with gentleness and reverence." This is where the English word *apologetics* comes from the Greek word translated *defense*. So we should learn some basic apologetics especially for the most common objections to Christianity. Certainly evolution would be first in the line of objections to Christianity and God. The simplest question to thwart evolution is "Where did the first molecule or atom come from?" You must start somewhere, and evolution must start with something, so where did that something come from?

Evolution

I was at work and discussing evolution with a co-worker, John. I was standing in the hall outside his office and saying that it takes more faith to believe in evolution than it takes to believe in God. As I was talking another co-worker was walking down the hall toward John's office. I had just learned through the Christian grapevine that the co-worker coming down the hall had just become a Christian, and I knew of him but didn't know him personally. As he approached, I simply said to John that you can ask anybody how to get to heaven, and they will tell you. So I stopped the new believer and asked him the question. His eyes got quite large and he showed signs of fear but responded boldly, "You must trust Christ as your personal savior." I still regret putting him on the spot, but John got the message.

Bible Reliability

A second common objection is the reliability of the Bible. Some comments you will get are:

- It was written by men; how could God be the author?
- The Bible was written 2000 years ago; it's not relevant today.
- It's confusing and too hard to understand.

First, the Bible is historically and scientifically accurate. Archeology has been a great support for Biblical accuracy. Whenever a new discovery is found, it is tested against the Bible, and over and over again the Bible proves to be true. It is also the most copied, most quoted, most commented about book in history. It is the only book that claims to be the Word of God. But if you just want to remember the best answer to the first question it is fulfilled prophecy. There are many prophecies already fulfilled, and there are about 300 concerning Christ. Skeptics would say that the prophecies in the Bible are too accurate and therefore must have been written after they occurred and not before. This was disproved with the discovery of the Dead Sea Scrolls which dated back to 100BC. Every book in the Old Testament was found except for Esther. So all the prophecies concerning Christ were dated back to at least 100 years before His birth.

Christ's Resurrection

Another common objection to Christianity is the resurrection of Christ. Skeptics would claim that it never happened, and the disciples probably stole the body. The greatest proof against this theory is the death of the disciples. Actually all but John were martyred for their faith, and none would renounce their faith in Christ. This in itself is not uncommon as many will die for what they believe to be true. But what is unique is that the disciples knew what was true. They were actually there, and nobody will die for a lie.

Then be diligent and study to be more effective, but again never be argumentative. We can discuss and to some degree debate but never argue. So as we build close spiritual relationships the best evangelistic style from *Becoming a Contagious Christian* would be the Intellectual Style. To demonstrate characteristics of the Intellectual style, you should be inquisitive, analytical, and logical. I know, your response is that you are not logical or analytical. That's just for engineers and geeks. That's ok, if you need help in this area get help, perhaps from your spouse, another Christian, or pastor. If their questions get too hard, just offer them your intellectual back up. Maybe you and your back up could meet with your friend with the questions. Remember it's your relationship with your friend that brought them to this point and not your intellectual ability.

Now our relationship is getting closer, and the spiritual discussions are getting deeper. Next let's look at building a deep spiritual relationship.

Small group discussion or personal reflection questions

1. List three common objections to Christianity from this chapter.

2. What is the most common objection to Christianity that you have seen?

3. What questions have you always struggled with?

   • How can you get them answered?

4. What questions have you been asked personally?

5. Tell about someone in your circle at this place in your relationship.

Chapter 8

"Seek After God"
Building Deep Spiritual
Relationships

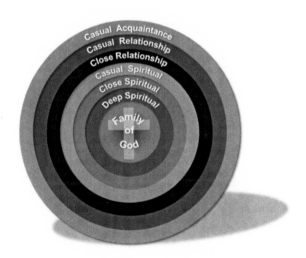

*W*e have had several spiritual discussions. Perhaps we have discussed some hard issues like "Why is there evil in the world?" or "Why does God allow us to suffer?" So they are at the point where they are intellectually interested, but because of their religious background or unreligious background they don't understand the concept of having a personal relationship with God. We need to help them experience God on a personal level not just an intellectual level. As they begin to experience God personally, and you share with them some of your experiences with God, your relationship with them will grow deeper.

Now is a good time to challenge them to SEEK God. II Chronicles 15:2b states, "And if you seek Him, He will let you find Him; but if you forsake Him, He will forsake you." Our pastor Lon Solomon tells his story about asking God for a Bible to read. He was broke and couldn't afford a Bible, but he told God if He would supply the Bible, Lon would read it. So God supplied it through a street evangelist. Lon read it and eventually put his faith in Christ.

When you challenge them, be careful to tell them to seek God with a humble heart and be fully open to God. We can't approach God with pride or arrogance and expect Him to respond, so humility is important. As I mentioned before we have a good friend Jamie Winship who had a unique way to start a spiritual conversation and to challenge people to seek God. He can build relationships quickly and go deep in just a short time. This is one time where Jamie builds relationships and challenges people to seek God on a plane flight back home.

Jamie writes:

So, we're flying back from Amman, Jordan to Atlanta, GA and I'm reading the Bible. I'm actually reading Isaiah 7 and am struck by the response of King Ahaz to God's offer in verses 10-13.

"Moreover, the Lord spoke again to King Ahaz, saying,

'Ask for yourself a sign (a token or proof) of the Lord your God [one that will convince you that God has spoken and will keep His word]; ask it either in the depth below or in the height above [let it be as deep as Sheol or as high as heaven].'

But Ahaz said, **'I will not ask, neither will I try the Lord.'**

And [Isaiah] said, 'Hear then, O house of David! Is it a small thing for you to **weary and try** the patience of men, but will you **weary and try** the patience of my God also?'"

Now here's some crazy irony: by being unwilling to *ask* and therefore *try* the Lord, Ahaz *wearies* and *tries* the Lord.

Conversely, then, it seems that the safest way to avoid *trying* the Lord is to *try* the Lord. The Bible is filled with stories of God asking people to avoid *trying* Him, by *trying* Him.

Now, I want to talk this over with someone, but Donna (Jamie's wife) is asleep and the passengers around me seem uninterested in engaging in deep meaningful conversations.

I want to try something. I want to find someone who doesn't yet know God but is willing to try and hear from Him.

I wander to the back of the plane and discover a group of flight attendants taking a break while normal passengers sleep.

One of the women, the elder of the group, asks if she can help me.

I feel a little uncomfortable, but I give it a try anyway. "I was wondering if any of you has ever heard God speak or wants to?"

Many of us would never ask a question like that because we would not want to try God, but the response of the flight crew was remarkable.

"I have at several points in my life," responds the older flight attendant. "They were by far the most beautiful times in my life."

A younger flight attendant says, "I have heard God, but I didn't listen." She begins to cry and walks away. The older flight attendant assures me the younger woman will be okay. "You've given me the courage to talk to her about things I should have talked with her about a year ago. Don't worry; I won't miss the opportunity again. Thanks."

I talk with the crew for over an hour. Perhaps when there is more time, I can relate their individual stories.

We land at JFK at 5:00 a.m. and need to quickly board the next flight to Atlanta. We have first class tickets, but I don't want to seclude ourselves there, but rather sit back in economy class where there are more people to talk with. I give our two tickets to two guys returning from tours in Afghanistan and take their tickets in exchange. Donna's ticket is in the exit row—nice—and mine is in the last row next to the toilets—perfect!

Fortunately, I'm surrounded by a wonderful Walton-like family heading out from upstate New York on their first vacation in years. The dad has been out of work for two years, but has just been hired by a great new company, so they're off to celebrate.

I am so excited to talk to them about the Lord. I'm sure they have heard His voice, and if they haven't, they have to be close. They are so nice. The dad introduces me to his wife and all the kids and as we ascend out of JFK, I'm raring to go.

But, then this guy comes walking down the aisle toward the restrooms and God says, "That guy. Talk to him?"

The guy in question is obviously a professional body-builder and he's wearing a Superman t-shirt. He draws a lot of attention as he walks toward the back of the plane, and I don't want to talk to him because he's massively ripped, visibly confident, and strikingly handsome.

"I like the Waltons better than Superman, Lord. Can't I just talk to them?"

Then it strikes me how much I am trying the Lord by not trying to talk to this guy.

I excuse myself from the Waltons and turn to face Superman who is bent over searching for a drink. I place my hand on his back causing him to whirl around.

"Are you okay?" I ask.

"Yes," he replies. "I just hate flying; it upsets my stomach. I was looking for some ginger-ale."

Now what do I say? I try what worked on the trans-Atlantic flight.

"Have you ever heard God speak?"

Superman seems dumbfounded. "I can't believe you asked me that," he says. "I have recently been told by doctors that I have a terminal heart disease that there is nothing they can do to correct. Sometime soon it will kill me."

Now I'm dumbfounded. "Have you ever thought of asking God to heal your heart?" I ask.

"No. God wouldn't do that for me. I'd be afraid to ask and try God's patience."

"Why?" I ask.

"Because, I have turned my back on God to worship my own body. I'm Jewish and I have ignored my Judaism. I can't suddenly turn back to God and ask for His help."

"You couldn't be more wrong about God," I tell him. "God is an expert in healing hearts. Why don't you try to listen to Him right now?"

"How?" he asks.

"I'll pray and you just listen, okay?"

"I'll try," he says

I place my hand on his shoulder and pray, "Lord, my friend here believes that because he has ignored You in his life that he cannot call out to You in his time of need. Will You just talk to him about that?"

We stand between the toilets and wait. Superman begins to shake his head. "This can't be God speaking," he says.

"Why? What's going through your mind?"

"I feel like God is telling me that every hour I have spent in a weight room, was an act of worship to Him. It's like even though I was doing it for selfish reasons God wants to use it for good. Does that make sense?"

"Yes," I say; chills puckering up and down my arms. "That's exactly how God talks. Ask God how He wants to use it for good."

Superman does this and we wait again.

"I can't believe this," he says.

"What?" I ask.

"God wants me to open a gym for kids in Palestine. That's insane. Doesn't God know I'm Jewish?"

We both laugh, and Superman tells me that this is the most exciting thing that has ever happened in his life. "This gives divine meaning to my whole life. I would love to help bring peace in the Middle East."

"There's just one thing," I say. "I'm pretty sure for this to happen you're going to need complete access to God through Jesus. What do you think of that?"

"If Jesus is the way to this kind of future, then I'm ready to accept him. How do I do that?"

"Invite Jesus into your life right now."

Right there, between the toilets somewhere over South Carolina, the Jewish Superman enters the Kingdom of God. Amen.

So Jamie has the unique gift to develop a relationship in a short time and encourage people to seek after God, but it's through a good spiritual conversation starter question and a strong caring attitude. Several years ago we had the privilege of walking the streets of Indonesia with them and watching as Jamie would engage the locals in conversation.

Challenge them to seek God and keep an environment with them where spiritual conversations are commonplace.

Our pastor Lon says, "Keep a consistent verbal witness to them, but don't hound them all the time."

I had a coworker, Lonnie, who I had this type of relationship with. I had had several spiritual conversations with Lonnie, and we could talk freely. Our discussions were always friendly and relaxed, but Lonnie wasn't ready to take that step of faith. So on a regular basis, not daily, I would simply say to Lonnie "are you ready to get saved today?" Lonnie would simply smile and say no, not today. He never got angry or say quit asking me. So I continued, until one day I asked the question, and he said yes. I was completely blown away. So I suggested we have lunch together. So we bought some sandwiches and went to a local park where Lonnie put his faith in Christ. He then walked the walk, and when his wife became ill with cancer he was able to lead her to the Lord. So keep spiritual conversations on going, again not stressful, but natural and relaxed.

Now spiritual conversations are ongoing, but your time together is limited. Perhaps you have several relationships at a similar place, and the need for spiritual discussions is increasing. One way to solve this problem is to start an evangelistic Bible study in your home.

On one Tuesday morning we had a rain delay for golf, and several of us golfers were hanging out in the pro shop. My normal procedure was to pray and see if God would have me talk to anyone. Most guys were in groups, but in the far corner of the pro shop stood a guy alone. I had never seen him before. So I approached him, started up a conversation, and invited him to my pre-golf Bible study on Mondays. He (Steve) then told me he recently went through major lung surgery, almost died in the process, and he needed some Bible study. But he wanted to have one in the evening.

This gave birth to an evening Bible study. We had our first meeting with no future obligations attached or commitments to continue. I think we had 3 or 4 guys. Steve and I were new in our relationship, but I had a relationship with two of the other guys. I think we first decided to go every other week and took a break for the first summer. Then they pushed for weekly meetings and never break. From this small beginning we have grown to 15-18 guys and all are not golfers. They are all in different places spiritually but love being in a group of men just doing life together around Biblical principles. God has gripped their hearts, and they are now doing the work of evangelists in our community.

As we build deep spiritual relationships the best evangelistic style from *"Becoming a Contagious Christian"* would be the Direct Style. Some characteristics of the direct style are confidence, assertive, and to-the-point. Again if you are not comfortable with this style and your relationships are at this point, get help. Maybe a friend or pastor from your church would be willing to lead an evangelistic Bible study if you did the inviting and hosting. Again remember, it's your relationship that brought them to this point not your direct style.

Now if you have a deep relationship and you are having ongoing spiritual discussions you need to have the tools to help them over the threshold and into the family of God.

Small group discussion or personal reflection questions

1. After your relationship with a friend grows deeper, it is time for you to encourage your friend to do what?

2. How would you answer the question, "Have you ever heard God speak?"

   • Try Jamie's spiritual conversation starter question on someone this week.

3. Who do you have in your life at this level?

4. When in your life did you seek after God, and He let you find Him?

   • Perhaps it was an answer to prayer – tell about that.

Chapter 9

"Build a Bridge"
Bringing Them into
the Family of God

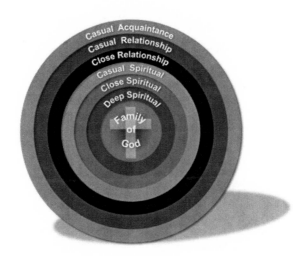

N ow if you have a deep relationship, and you are having ongoing spiritual discussions, you need to have the tools to help them over the threshold and into the family of God. You are having on going spiritual conversations and your friend asks you about your story and that's when you panic. I Peter 3:15a states: "Always be prepared to give an answer to everyone who asks you to give the reason for the hope that you have" (NIV). So let's get prepared. First let's look at some basic principles in telling your story.

The best approach is to break your story into three parts. Part 1: What was your life like before Christ (BC)? Part 2: How did you come to meet Christ (MC)? Part 3: What has your life been like after Christ (AC)? So while you are thinking about your story, I'll tell you mine.

BC (Before Christ)

In my early childhood I don't remember going to church. But somewhere around the time I was eleven or twelve we started to attend a small country church. I was placed into a boys Sunday school class, and I can remember the teacher saying that good boys go to heaven and bad boys don't. I guess he was trying to scare us into good behavior. That began my search to learn about God, because if what he said was true we all have to be good every hour of the day or night. How difficult would that be? Also at that time I can remember adults joking about heaven and hell saying that they didn't want to go to heaven because all of their friends would be in hell. Anyway it put a fear in me that if hell existed, I sure didn't want to go there. So after about five years trying to learn about God, I came to understand that no one deserves heaven by being good because we just can't be good enough.

MC (Met Christ)

At the age of seventeen I started to date Carol, and I was only allowed out on a date once a week. Sometimes that once a week date was going with her to church on Sunday night. It was during one of the church dates that I put my faith in Christ as my Lord and Savior.

Her high school youth group would completely run the Sunday evening service once a quarter, I think the fifth Sunday of the month. So at one of these services the speaker called for a recommitment of the Christian teens and to come forward and make it public. Carol was in the choir, and she went down with many other teens. Since this didn't apply to me, I didn't move but stayed in the pews with everyone else. But then he gave an invitation for those who wanted to trust in Christ, and I went down. This was not the first time I had heard the gospel. But it was the first time I responded. I had heard and understood it before at least once at a winter church camp, and I was concerned about giving my life to Christ. Maybe God would want me to be a missionary in Africa and going to Africa did not sound appealing to me. So after I wrestled with that thought and concluded that God knows me best, and if that is what He wanted me to do, I would do it. So that night I went forward, and there, among all the other teens, I prayed to put my total dependence on Jesus for my salvation.

AC (After meeting Christ)

After my decision to put my faith in Christ, I continued to seek to learn about God. We got involved in every church we attended over the years and served in many different areas. Even though life has its different seasons God has been faithful, and I have never desired to go back and change my decision. I have had the privilege to be on staff at a church and to serve God in all aspects of my life. And as I get older and my body starts to reflect that, eternity in heaven continues to look better and better.

So that's my story. Take time now and write down your story. Remember the three parts:

1. **BC – Your life before Christ**
2. **MC – How you met Christ**
3. **AC – Your life after Christ**

Maybe your story doesn't have three parts because you came to Christ at an early age. That's ok. Just focus on how you came to Christ and your life afterward. So write it now and tell it to a Christian friend later for practice. Then you will be ready to tell it when God gives you the opportunity.

Don't devalue your story no matter how simple it is! Chuck Swindoll said in his book *Come Before Winter* the skeptic may deny your doctrine or attack your church, but he cannot honestly ignore the fact that your life has changed. Remember, your friend will be interested in your story because it's your story, and you have a relationship with them. So learn to tell your story, and then be ready to share the gospel message.

There are many ways to share the gospel but you don't need to learn all of them, just one that you are comfortable with. One gospel illustration is the Bridge. This requires a paper and pencil which can be a drawback but it is a good illustration of how we are separated from God and only Christ can bridge the gap between us and God.

The first step in the Bridge Illustration is to draw a picture that shows **US** on one side and **GOD** on the other. Then say that we have become separated from God because of our

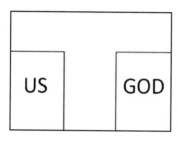

sin. You can explain that we were once walking with God, but because we all have sinned starting with Adam, we are now separated. Now add to the original picture by drawing **arrows** from the **US** side toward the bottom between **US** and **GOD**.

While you are drawing say that we attempt to get to God by doing good things but we fall way short. God requires perfection, and we can't be perfect; so we fall short, and the penalty for our sin is death. Now draw the word **DEATH** at the bottom to show where we are destined to go. Then say

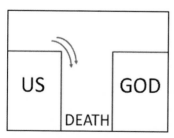

that because of falling short, we will be eternally separated from **GOD**.

Next draw a large **cross** that bridges the gap between **US** and **GOD**. While drawing this say, but the good news is that God did for us what we couldn't do

for ourselves, by building a bridge back to Him. God did this through Christ by dying on the cross as our substitute. Christ paid the spiritual death penalty that we owed and rose from the dead so that we might have eternal life. Then draw an **arrow** from the **US** side to **GOD** and put an **X** through

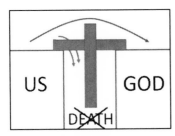

the word **DEATH** and say, it's not good enough to know that Christ died for us, we must put our faith and trust on Him by admitting that we have sinned and ask for His forgiveness. As we put our faith in Christ, we cross over the bridge to **GOD** and are no longer destined for eternal **DEATH** but will spend eternity with **GOD** in heaven.

The one that I have used over the years is the A-B-C illustration. I simply say that getting to heaven is as easy as A-B-C.

A – We must <u>A</u>dmit that we are a sinner. Verses to use are Romans 3:23, "for all have sinned and fall short of the glory of God," and Romans 3:10 "There is none righteous not even one." Actually sin means to miss the mark. It's like trying to hit a dime with a bow and arrow at 50 yards every day of your life and never miss. So we all miss the mark and fall short of God's perfection and therefore don't deserve heaven.

B – We must <u>B</u>elieve that Christ died for our sins and put our faith in Him. A good verse to use is John 3:16, "For God so loved the world, that He gave His only begotten Son, that whoever believes in Him shall not perish, but have eternal life." Only those who believe in Christ have eternal life. This is not merely an intellectual agreement, but to believe means to put your complete trust in Christ to save you. It's like knowing that a specific chair is strong enough to support you, but when you go and sit in the chair then you are fully trusting that it will hold you up. In the same way we must completely rest in Christ and not lean on ourselves.

C – We must *C*all upon God to save us. A good verse is Romans 10:9, "that if you confess with your mouth Jesus as Lord, and believe in your heart that God raised Him from the dead, you will be saved." We can simply pray to God and admit we are a sinner and tell Him we are totally putting our faith in Jesus to save us.

Learn to tell your story and also to give a gospel presentation, then be ready because God will give you opportunity to use both.

In chapter 6 we talked about inviting them to church related activities. Perhaps your church has a basic Christianity class, we call ours Christianity 101. Through a series of classes the gospel is explained in detail, and it is a great environment to address any objections they might have. If you have such a class, perhaps you could invite your friend, and you two could take the class together. Then you will be there to help answer questions he or she might have.

We need to be ready to help them cross the line of faith and come into the family of God. Next let's look at some other specific ways we can build relationships in our community.

Small group discussion or personal reflection questions

1. What is your story:

BC – Your life before Christ

MC – How you met Christ

AC – Your life after you met Christ

- Practice your story with your small group or a Christian friend.

2. Which gospel presentation will you choose to learn? Bridge

A-B-C

- Practice your presentation with your small group or a Christian friend.

Chapter 10

"Making Friends"
Relational Evangelism
In the Community

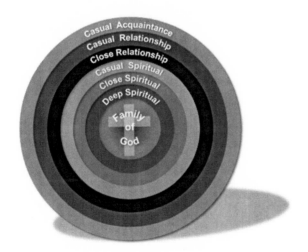

*I*n our busy, hectic lifestyle we don't take time to get to know our neighbors. Our schedule is filled by our jobs, children, and church which are all important. But we, as members of the body of Christ, are missing the opportunities to evangelize in our neighborhoods. As I said in the introduction, David Jeremiah states, "The greatest untapped harvest fields in modern America are our neighborhoods." If our communities are untapped, how do we reach them? Again we must first build casual relationships through secular group activities. Therefore I would like to give you some ideas that you might use in your own community.

Golf

I know, I have mentioned golf quite often. But it worked for me, and it could work for you too. Even if you don't live in a golf community, you could organize a regular golf outing to a local course for people in your community. I started relational evangelism around golf. Our community was new and growing, and our normal weekly men's golf league/outing grew from 20 to 80 in a couple of years. During hours on the golf course, I got to know many guys. We had our time together in which the relationships grew, and I was able to have many spiritual conversations. After building one-on-

one relationships, the next step God used in the golf relationship process, was to start a pre-golf Bible study. This beginning was not without opposition. After I announced the beginning of the Bible study, I was told that we could not have a Bible study in the clubhouse. But God provided a way through our club pro, and we started in his office.

Walking

You could start a walking group or simply walk with a neighbor. This is what Marissa, a good friend from church did.

Marissa Writes:

Over the years I have prayed for a woman in my neighborhood. I knew she did not attend church with her husband and daughters. Three years ago, the empty nest hit me pretty hard. I prayed for a friend. Soon after, I ran into this woman. She complained about gaining a lot of weight. I invited her to walk with me every day. She accepted the invitation. We have been walking for one hour at least five days per week. Our relationship started growing instantly. I learned that her spiritual education began and ended with being baptized as an infant.

I also learned that she loves musicals. Not so coincidentally, I knew that my next door neighbors' young son was performing in a musical at a theater close by. I invited her to go with me, explaining beforehand that the musical, *Children of Eve*, was going to be about a Bible story. She still agreed to go and really enjoyed it. The musical was about the creation story up to Noah and the flood. However, I took the opportunity to point out how the story in the musical differed from the Bible. That raised her curiosity, so she borrowed her husband's Bible to read the book of Genesis.

Because I learned that she also loves archeology, I informed her there was an Archeology Study Bible. She bought it and has found it interesting. I would love to say that she spends all her spare time reading it, but I cannot. In this area, I have had to practice patience. But I was not deterred. I invited her to attend a weekly women's Bible study with me at McLean Bible Church. She agreed. We are now starting our fourth study. Presently, she watches the internet broadcast of McLean Bible Church every Sunday, and thoroughly enjoys the preaching of our pastor, Lon Solomon. Although the concept of walking by faith is difficult for her, she is reading *The Case for Faith*, by Lee Strobel.

Our relationship has gone through most of the relationship stages. We have become close friends, and she is now comfortable asking me questions about Christianity. What a privilege God has given me to share the faith!

Biking

Exercise continues to be an important part of American life and starting or being involved in a biking group could be an effective way to build relationships. If you are a biker or you know that some of your neighbors are bikers, just try it to see if God can use it.

Game Night

Chris is starting a men's Christian discussion group through relationships developed through an adult game night in their community. Someone else actually started the game night, and he and his wife just got involved. Now their neighbors are on their hearts, and he has taken the next step. His first activity is to read a book on raising daughters together since all the men in the group have daughters.

Movie Night

Another idea is a kid's movie night. The rising cost of movie tickets today could make this an attractive event. Invite the neighborhood kids over for pizza and a movie. Just try one first, and then if it is successful, try another. You could also invite the parents and make it a family movie night. Pick a good clean movie, not necessarily Christian, which would be interesting and enjoyable to your neighbors and their children.

Volunteer Work

Volunteer opportunities can be a great way to make relationships. Larry, a good friend, volunteers at a local hospital and with voter registration. I'm sure there are many other opportunities in your community such as after school programs or volunteering in the library. With a little leg work you could find something that fits your interest and schedule.

Other opportunities in our community have been the community chorale group, community players (acting), dine out groups, and neighborhood cook outs/dinners. If your community doesn't have any group activities, you need to be proactive and start one. This is a very important first step.

Small group discussion or personal reflection questions

1. What new relationships have you built through community activities?

    • What was the activity?

    • Who is your new acquaintance?

2. If you are not involved in a community activity now, which one interests you?

    • How can you make it part of your life?

3. Do you have a skill or knowledge in some area that you could use to create a community activity? If so, what is it?

Chapter 11

"God is at Work
Where You Work"
Relational Evangelism
In the Work Place

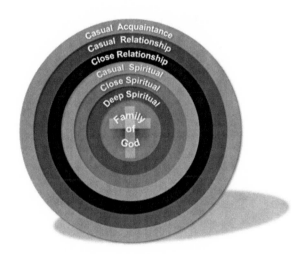

*V*iewing your job as a ministry will help you through difficult times at work and help you to prioritize the importance of impacting lives. Most of us interface with many people through our daily jobs. As we spend time with people, we can build relationships that God can use to bring people into the kingdom. Our job then is the group activity by which we build casual relationships. Building close relationships then can naturally happen through the normal one-on-one activities within our workplace. Building spiritual relationships can be difficult, depending upon the freedom you have within your workplace environment.

One of the overriding principles that God impressed on me was that to be obedient in having spiritual conversations requires sacrifice. It seemed like every time I was working to meet a dead line or just busy doing the task at hand, someone would come by and want to talk. I had to set aside what I was doing, without impacting any work, and focus on him. So if we are willing to make the sacrifice, God will give us the opportunity.

Actually, as I reflect upon my time in the corporate world, I had many opportunities to have spiritual discussions; but the results were not as I would have expected. If you would have asked me at the beginning of my business life who would be most receptive to the gospel message I would have said: first, my peers; second, my bosses; and third, my employees. After looking back I found it was just the opposite. My peers were the least receptive, and my employees the most. I'm not sure why, maybe it's like the gasoline engine story I told you in chapter 4.

On one occasion I was a first line manager, and a peer manager in the same organization started telling my employees that I was not doing a very good job. At first I was defensive and told them not to talk to him, but God convinced me that He could handle it, so I told them to go ahead and talk to him. My peer manager was trying to move up the corporate ladder, and he viewed me as one of the rungs. But God worked it out that instead of acquiring my business area, he had difficulty with his; and our superiors gave his business area to me. This was sort of like the story in the book of Esther about Esther and Haman. (If you have never read or don't remember the story, take time to read Esther, an Old Testament book which tells about how God works through the small circumstances.)

As he saw his job falling apart, he came into my office one day and closed the door. I can still picture him walking back and forth in my small office as he struggled with the fact that his career was not working out as he planned. He then stopped and looked at me and asked, "What should I do?" I replied that I'm not sure exactly what the answer is, but I know where to find it, and I pointed to my Bible on my credenza. He then puffed out his chest and said "Oh, Yeah." He then walked toward my Bible, and I can remember saying to God in my mind, "Ok, it's in your hands." He then opened my Bible to a random page, pointed down and read, "Better is a poor man who walks in his integrity than he who is perverse in speech and is a fool" (Proverbs 19:1). It was so powerful that he fell slightly backward and looked at me and said, "Maybe the answers are there." I lost track of him after that as he transferred out, but I hope by now he has taken the most important step and trusted Christ.

Peers can be a difficult mission field, but I found that employees were the most receptive. On one occasion I was traveling to Austin with an employee, Rich; we both got upgrades to business class and were seated side by side. I had brought along my new evangelistic Bible and thought this would be a good time to try it out. So all the way from Washington D.C. to Austin I keep trying the questions on Rich from my Bible. Rich and I had talked before, but this was intense even for me. So we got to the hotel in Austin, and I went up to my room, but Rich stayed down at the bar to crash. While at the bar he met a woman and proceeded to complain about his boss reading the Bible to him on the trip down. After listening for a while, the woman then said that she was a Christian and liked the Bible. Well, to make a long story short, Rich became a Christian, married the woman, and moved to Austin.

As you have the opportunity, continue to use good bridge statements to have spiritual conversations without crossing the line of appropriateness. On one occasion I might have crossed over that line with an employee. We were in the process of testing some newly designed hardware and had to work around the clock to meet our schedule. Sometimes the stress between the shifts can be high which almost resulted in a physical fight between two of my employees. As I came in that morning I immediately met with the aggressor in my office and explained to him that I could fire him on the spot for this kind of behavior. He had a hard time calming down and finally agreed to apologize to his coworker. He then stated that his home life wasn't going very well, and his marriage was on the rocks. So his job was in trouble as well as his home, so I thought that only God could solve this mess. So I went through the gospel with him at risk of losing my job; but after I was done, he looked at me and said that he was doing ok and didn't need God. But still employees were usually the most receptive.

Sometimes relationships in the workplace can lead to a personal ongoing relationship that God can use, but be sensitive to your employer; and, if necessary, talk only at break times and in break locations. I asked Monica a church friend and member of our MBC small group to tell about a coworker.

Monica tells her story:

I always worried I was not doing "my job" as a believer in Jesus Christ by not leading anyone to Christ. I know I was able to share with children at church during the AWANA program, but not with my peers. No way, that whole idea intimidated me! It was too uncomfortable for me. I'd ask myself. . .What if my sharing changed the way the relationship worked? What if I was now deemed an outsider? Or what if they thought I was just plain weird? I now understand God is working through me, despite my hang-ups and fears. I was also concerned about not being academic or intelligent enough to defend what I believe. I now say, "HOGWASH!" God is more than able to use my feeble attempts, and He does. It's never about me anyway; it's always about Him. All God has asked me, asked all of us, is to be who He has created us to be. He will do the rest!

For me, what God has done to help me share my faith is place me in situations where I naturally share Him. One example is at work. I've had a co-worker at work for several years, and we worked together as teammates. She understood from my work and life choices that they were based on my faith in God. Many of our conversations over several years were pretty superficial; what we did over the weekend; what we did for entertainment;

what we did for vacation; nothing from the really deep parts of life. However, what I found was when something really hard to deal with in life hit her; she came to me and cried (after a six year relationship). She was not normally someone who cried. She poured out her heart, and I said I would pray for her because "I" did not have any answers!

What I saw God do was quietly open the door after all those years. We didn't have any close contact after that incident for a while, but in the meantime God did what God does best. He softened her heart. She told me later that the prayer comforted her because someone "bigger" than she was would help shoulder her burden. We were not close friends, but after that incident God started drawing us together.

Another factor that helped open the door to God was when she took up a hobby that I was already involved in. It has given us a common ground and more opportunity to have deeper conversations. We train together to run in races, and it is during those moments that we have some of our deepest conversations. . .about life. . . about God. He gives me an opportunity in those moments to talk about what it means to have a faith in God. Why I make certain choices because of my faith. As she works through the training and an incredibly hard patch in life, she is more willing to open up about the intimate/deep parts of her life. The parts that people normally keep concealed. As she opens up, I often have to tell her I don't have an answer, but I tell her what the Bible says about that type of situation, or I share how I used biblical precepts/principals to solve a similar problem. She'll make a comment or ask a question, and I'll answer it as best I can. I don't fret over my answer because I know if I am attempting to use God's word then it won't return void. I don't have to quote scripture verbatim, but I may say something like, "there is a verse in the Bible that says something like this. . ." and I'll paraphrase it so she'll glean the meaning out of it. Sometimes I'll say "because of my faith" or "I am going to go 'religious' on you. . ." to let her know the thoughts or words coming out aren't from me but from God's world view.

I feel because I am not "preaching" at her, she is able to take or leave the information I shared. It seems like since I did not tell her what to do; she'll take the time to process it, and then come back later and ask more questions. I have found that if I am vulnerable and genuine, she will continue to be open to God's Word. I don't hammer her with truth, but share openly, candidly about what God has done and what God is currently doing in my life. I also feel because I respect her, she shows respect to my world view. I also know that I am the only person she knows who was raised with a faith or has an active faith in Jesus Christ. I try to show that I don't have to be perfect or know all the answers. I have also demonstrated when I have a weakness how I handle it because of my faith.

One time at work someone did something that really bothered me, and I started to gossip about it during lunch. After lunch when I went to my desk and the Holy Spirit convicted me of what I had just done. . .sinned! What I love about God is He gave me the opportunity later that same afternoon to admit my sin to the teammate (the unbeliever) while we were training; and in that simple moment of weakness, I was able to tell her that is why I need a savior! I often think that God uses us best when we are most willing to show our weaknesses! In that moment without my planning it, or rehearsing it, or fretting over it, God gave me the opportunity to share His good news. We need a savior because of sin, and He has given us one in Jesus Christ! I wish I could say that she has accepted Christ as her Savior; it hasn't happened yet, but she has been willing to go to a conference with me at church. I think it was the second time in her life she was in a church. What I have learned about this journey is that as long as we are faithful in trying to share His good news, HE will finish the job with the right amount of finesse!

Remember your job can be your ministry opportunity. This is especially important to remember when the stress and pressure of the job become difficult. For years I kept a sketch on my office wall by Joni Erickson Tada. The verse in the sketch was John 7:38, "He that believes on me out of him will flow rivers of living water." Joni was a constant reminder to me that I didn't have it so tough, and my ministry to people was more valuable than my job.

Okay, back to work! ☺ Let's now see what we can do in the church.

Small group discussion or personal reflection questions

1. Tell about some workplace relationships and where they are in the relationship scale.

2. What are some ways that you can create one-on-one conversation opportunities at work?

3. Do you know of other Christians in your workplace with whom you can partner to reach your coworkers?

   • Who are they, and what is their spiritual background?

Chapter 12

"Reaching Out" Relational Evangelism In the Church

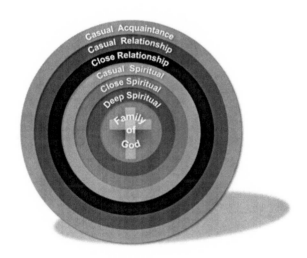

*I*n today's environment all evangelistic thrusts within the church should be evaluated on their ability to build relationships with people outside the church. Some churches are making very good progress in this area, and these are just a few examples or ideas that you might try in your church.

Low Income Communities

At McLean Bible Church (Prince William Campus) we have an ongoing ministry to a low income community. We actually take a food truck into the community to give out food where it's needed. As we go, we ask for prayer requests and see if there are other needs that we can meet. We also have started a tutoring ministry to the school students in the community. We supply the computers necessary to make it happen and meet with them regularly to help with their school assignments. The purpose of this helpful hand in the community is to build relationships in order to have spiritual conversations.

Assisted living book club – Monica writes:

Our church started a ministry at an assisted living facility. The premise was to give the residents the opportunity to hear God's word at a church service performed at the facility. Many of the residents are not able to leave the facility due to health issues, which means they lose the ability to worship and hear God's word on a regular basis. Several of the church members started to serve at the facility on a rotating basis (about once a month). It was quickly shown to me that it would be hard to share Christ with residents seeing them only once a month during the service. The focus on Sunday was the sermon, and many residents were not able to do more than sit and listen. I wanted to afford more of an opportunity to interact with the residents. I thought a book club might be the answer to the dilemma. Right now in our culture a popular social activity is starting a book club in which everyone reads the same book and then discusses it. My idea was to use books by Christian authors that would hopefully lead to discussions on life issues, God's truth, and faith in Jesus Christ. I thought that if I started a Bible study many would not attend because of the effort a study would require. I also wanted to see if a book club would draw in seekers and non-believers into the mix. A book club might be more acceptable to those who are outside the church. Since the meetings were in an assisted living facility, I read one to two chapters aloud to the residents at each meeting, and then we talked about it.

What I saw happen was amazing! I would pray before I went into the facility asking God to give me His words and His wisdom in what to say to the group. I may or may not prepare questions ahead of time to discuss. What I experienced was how God always brought the conversations back to Him. The first book was historical fiction during WWII. We would discuss things like how society and the church lost its voice in Germany. I'd ask questions like, "Do we see those types of events happening now?" I was delighted by their insight and ability to articulate their thinking. We discussed how important it was to know truth and be able to stand up for it in adversity. What I liked about the experience was that we began our time together reading, discussing, but then somehow we would fall into sharing some of the nominal things that were happening in each of our lives. I didn't plan the personal interactions; they just started happening naturally. After a while, in order to draw the evening to a close, I would ask if there was anything that they needed prayer for; at first they did not know how to respond. I gave a few examples of what I do in my own life and then tentatively they would share one or two prayer requests with me. A few weeks passed by, and as soon as I walked in one of the participants popped-up with, "You won't believe it, but God answered the prayers I asked you about!" She was so excited. She was a nominal Christian, someone that had grown up in the Christian tradition, but whose faith in God was not always evident. I understood at that point that God was working in the group, and His presence would grow stronger as time passed. What was great was even though a particular book did not have Christian themes, having a faith in God always seemed to seep into the conversation.

Many times the theme in the book would bring up thought provoking questions: Is there truly a heaven? Or hell? Why is there evil in the world? What can we do to stop the derogation of our culture and society? Often they would ask me questions, and I would go home research the answers and come back to the next meeting with an answer to their questions from the Bible. Several times I said, "Next time bring your Bible, and we'll look up the Scripture I found to answer your questions." Once after they asked me about being able to lose your salvation, God gave me the very answer to the question, and I didn't even have to do the research. My pastor preached a sermon on that very topic that week. I asked the book club members if I could bring in my computer so they could listen to the pastor's answers on CD. They were very open to the idea and the next week I brought in the computer so they could hear his answer to their question. One of the ladies asked many questions about heaven and not being able to lose your salvation. In this environment life can pass unexpectedly, and she needed reassurance. She is now with the Lord, and I am happy to say it is because of the book club that she confidently made it into the Kingdom!

Over time I felt that we all looked forward to the life sharing part as much or more than the book sharing part of the meeting. We began to share deeper life experiences, and the prayer requests became less superficial and more from the cares of their souls. My purpose in creating the book club was to bless the residents of the facility, but what I found was I was blessed as much if not more by the time I spent with the group. I learned through this experience that I should not be afraid to build relationships with people outside my comfort zone. I now see how God will give the words, and the Holy Spirit will do the work in me, and in the other person(s). The only thing I am asked to do is share my heart for God, invite others into that same type of relationship, and then watch God work. As I saw with the population at the assisted living facility, time is of the essence. What are you waiting for?

This assisted living ministry continues to grow as we are now in two different assistant living facilities and lead other activities during the week such as sing alongs, game night, and Bible studies. These smaller groups help the relationship building process and provide one-on-one opportunities with these precious people. Also at McLean Bible Church we started "The House" in the inner city of Washington D.C. At "The House" teens can meet for fun, relationship building, and Bible study. The House is an oasis in a difficult community and provides a safe haven for kids. The leaders there have shown such love to those kids that many have come to know Christ.

Most evangelical efforts we do in the church today should begin with the idea of building relationships. If it's a contact, how do we follow-up? What is the next step and the step after that? How do we move them through the relationship circles? Ongoing personal relationships are necessary in having successful evangelistic efforts.

The ideas and possibilities are endless. The people of Tristate Fellowship in Hagerstown, MD create and distribute Valentine gift boxes to widows and widowers and do home-help jobs for the elderly, all with the intent of building meaningful relationships with the people they meet. They also have a couple of programs that focus on the homeless. For one they work at the REACH shelter and build relationships where some have come to church as a result. Second a program called "Homeless for Housing" which helps supply needs such as home furnishings and cookware to a family going from a homeless situation to living in their own home. At MBC we do a turkey outreach every Thanksgiving and give out several thousand dinners to needy families.

So think of ways your church can reach into the community to build relationships in order to have the privilege of sharing the gospel with them.

Small group discussion or personal reflection questions

1. What does your church do in the area of relational evangelism?

2. What ministries in the chapter are of interest to you?

3. How could you start some type of relational evangelism ministry?

   - Through your community or Sunday school group

   - Through your small group

Chapter 13

"Overcoming the Physical" Relational Evangelism In the Family

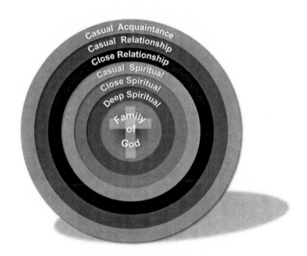

F amilies are probably the most difficult mission field. Broken relationships within the family are on the rise, and to be able to restore those relationships in order to have spiritual conversations can be difficult, but they are not impossible. The USA has become a nation of broken families. The growth in the number of children born into broken families grew from 12% in 1950 to 58% in 1992, and has continued to grow. Certainly divorce continues to be the major cause of the brokenness, but it's not the only one. Our pastor Lon Solomon grew up in a strict Jewish home, and after becoming a Christian he was essentially an outcast. But through prayer and persistence God was able to overcome the brokenness. Lon tells his story, taken from his book *the 23RD psalm for the 21st century.*

Lon writes:

It has been said that if you are Jewish, you can only grow up to be one of three things; a doctor, a lawyer, or a failure. By that definition I fall into the final category. You see, my story is about how a nice Jewish boy from Portsmouth, Virginia, ended up as the pastor of a big evangelical church in McLean, Virginia. A Jewish pastor might sound strange, but then again, my story could read as a Hollywood screenplay.

I was born and raised in Portsmouth, Virginia, by Conservative Jewish parents. My dad grew up in a very religious home; my mom did not. My dad's parents were from the "old country" (Europe). My grandfather was from Romania and my grandmother from Germany. According to family lore, they met as teenagers on the boat coming to America, fell in love and got married. My dad's parents were strongly Orthodox. I remember as a young child watching my grandmother prepare the *Shabbat* (Sabbath) meal before sundown each Friday. My grandparents left the light switches on in their home so as not to violate the rabbinic rules about "lighting a fire" on the Sabbath. They walked to the synagogue instead of driving, an activity prohibited on the Sabbath.

My parents were not nearly as religious. Like many others, they saw religion as an obligation and not a way to know God personally. We never had a Bible in our home. We did not sit down and pray together before meals; in fact we didn't pray at all. We lit candles every Sabbath, went to the High Holiday services at *Rosh Hashanah* and *Yom Kipper*, and had a Passover *seder* meal in our home. But the presence of God was not a reality in our lives.

After coming to Christ Lon's life changed dramatically, and through prayer, persistence and patience God worked. He continues his story:

However, my Jewishness continued to be an important part of my identity. And my desire to see my Jewish family know the Messiah never waned. One of the greatest privileges God has ever given me was leading my dad to Jesus just before he died. He had a heart condition and was taken to the hospital in Charlottesville,

North Carolina. By this time he had already had three heart attacks. My mother called to tell me, "Your dad's in the hospital with hepatitis. He's really ill and you need to come and see him." She made it sound so serious that I rushed down that day to see him, praying all the way.

By this time I had been a Christian for seven years. I had shared Jesus with him multiple times over those years, but he had routinely ignored me. In my frustration, the Lord spoke to me and said, "Lon, remember what Cora told you. It's prayer that will bring the power of the Holy Spirit into his heart." So I began to talk less and pray more for him – begging God to bring him to faith in Jesus before the next heart attack killed him.

I walked into the hospital room and my dad was sitting bold upright, eating a banana! I couldn't believe my mom had misled me and there he was, doing fine. I guess that's what comes from having a Jewish mother.

We started to talk about the weather and I could tell something was on his mind. After we exchanged a few more pleasantries, he said' "You know, Lon, I've been doing a lot of thinking lately."

"Well Dad, thinking is good. It's good to think." "I've been thinking a lot about the stuff you've been telling me about Jesus.'

Oh my, I thought, holding my breath.

"I am beginning to wonder if maybe everything you are telling me is right."

I couldn't believe what I was hearing, I had been praying for my dad every day, sometimes twice a day. And suddenly I wondered, *Could my prayers be answered?* I felt like calling the nurse and asking her to clear the bed in the next room for me. *Lord please don't let me say something wrong here,* I prayed silently.

"There is no doubt in my mind that I'm right," I told my dad, but you've never been interested or wanted to talk about this. Why all of a sudden are you saying I'm right?"

"Well, Lon, I've got to tell you," he replied, "I know I'm a sick man, and I decided that I could find everything in Orthodox Judaism The idea of dying terrified him. After his heart attack, my mom later told me that he would stay up all night walking the halls, terrified that if he fell asleep, he'd never wake up. "I finally walked out of the synagogue after Yom Kipper services. " he continued, "I stood on the front steps of the synagogue and said to myself, *I don't have any more assurance of what's going to happen to me after I die now than I did before I went through all the ritual. Maybe Lon is right.*"

"Dad, I am so sure I am right, it's not even funny," I said. The next morning I had the privilege of getting down on my knees with my father, next to the hospital bed, and praying with him as he asked Jesus into his life. He died one week later, to the day. During that week, his number one issue was that he believed Jesus had given him the assurance of eternal life, but he did not want to stop being Jewish. I tried to explain, "Dad, you don't become a Gentile when you believe in Jesus! You're always Jewish! You just complete everything that being Jewish is all about!"

The last time I saw my father before he died, he was in intensive care, hooked up to a tracheal tube. He had suffered his fourth (and final) heart attack while still in the hospital. He wasn't able to talk and frantically wanted to tell me something. There was a piece of paper, covered in plastic, with the alphabet written on it, so that patients could spell out words. He reached for this piece of paper and spelled out "L-O-R-D" "A-N-D" "J-E-W" I knew he was saying, "Lon I have the Lord in my life, but I'm still a Jew." It was so affirming to see that, even under all the sedatives, my dad had enough presence of mind to say, "I know exactly who I am, Lon, and I've got Jesus Christ in my life."

My brother was next to come to faith. I'd shared what I believe with him many times, but it was his wife, Patrice, who eventually led him to Christ. While visiting her sister in Texas, Patrice attended a revival meeting at her sister's church and asked Jesus into her life. When she came back home and shared the good news, my brother accepted Jesus as his Lord and Savior. To this day he is walking with the Lord.

My brother and I began to double-team my mom. She had been battling breast cancer for some time when my brother finally led her to a relationship with Jesus. He called me up and said, "You'll never guess what's happened. I've led mom to Christ. "I said, "That's awesome! I'm really glad you got to do it, since I led Dad to Christ." It was gracious of the Lord to give each of us one of them. Like my dad, she had been terrified of dying. Right after I hung up the phone, I called my mom and said "I understand you have asked Jesus to be your Lord and Savior." She said, "Yes I did and I know I am going to heaven now. Isn't that true?" And I said, "Oh mom, that is so utterly true, it's not even funny." I had a wonderful time praying with her over them telephone. She died just a few weeks later.

Lon's story can also be yours, if you continue to reestablish broken relationships. Like Lon said, "Don't give up on them." A few years ago my granddaughter and daughter got me connected to a family internet site. I would look on the site when a picture of me was posted or maybe some comment of years past, but I was not an active participant. Then my cousin, actually my third cousin, starting saying things about me when we were growing up, as we used to hang out a lot but haven't had much contact since we were kids. He was saying things like "You saved my life when we were kids," and "my life is now your responsibility," something like that. I vaguely remembered that time as we were quite young. But as I remember we were swimming in a public pool, and he jumped into the deep end but stayed at the bottom of the pool. So I went and got help, and they dove in and pulled him out.

The experience was far more memorable to him than to me, and he kept talking about it. So I took it as an invitation to get together. He still lived close to the town where we grew up, and on one occasion when Carol and I went back to visit family, I met with him for breakfast. I quickly found out that he was as far from Christianity as you can get, a devout atheist. But because of our old existing relationship we could talk freely about spiritual things. I gave him some things to consider and later he wanted to hear my <u>whole</u> story. Then I had the privilege to go through the gospel, and I added him to my daily prayer list. He now calls me his missionary cousin and refers to himself as my agnostic cousin, who is open to the existence of God. I continue to pray for him every day, and we connect when we can even though we are separated by hundreds of miles.

People today are reconnecting to old family members or friends because of the societal relationship void and social networking sites. So maybe you can reconnect. Your life has changed because of Christ, and now you can go back and reconnect to old family or friends in order to point them to God.

Small group discussion or personal reflection questions

1. Do you pray for a family member who doesn't know Christ?

   - Who is he or she?

   - Where is your relationship with him or her?

   - How can you move him or her along the relationship scale?

2. Is there some family member or friend from your past with whom you can reconnect?

   - Who is he or she?

   - How can you reconnect?

Chapter 14

Let's Review

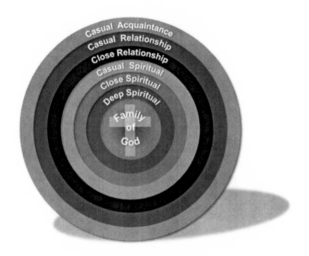

*T*he most important truth to take away from this book is that we must be PROACTIVE in making relationships with unbelievers. As our relationships grow closer, we should have more frequent and deeper spiritual conversations. Each step in the relationship process requires us to take some action. Relationships by themselves will not naturally grow deeper and closer. Spiritual conversations are not common; they require relationship groundwork to help make them easy and natural. From the relationship model the first step is Building Casual Relationships since we already have many acquaintances.

Building Casual Relationships

- Go where the fish are – get involved in secular group activities
- Use an Interpersonal Style

We need to go and get involved in non-church activities. For some of us our work place already applies but what about our communities? What activity in your community can you create or just get plugged into? Again the best style from *Becoming a Contagious Christian* is the Interpersonal

Style. We need to be a friend. This applies to all relationship levels, but it's especially important here.

Building Close relationships

- Try one-on-one activities
- See where God is at work
- Start an Evangelism Budget
- Use a Serving Style

As we see where God is at work we should look to serve Him by serving unbelievers where possible. Paul stated in II Corinthians 5:18b, "God reconciled us to Himself through Christ and gave us the ministry of reconciliation. " John MacArthur states, "This speaks to the reality that God wills sinful men to be reconciled to Himself. God has called believers to proclaim the gospel of reconciliation to others. The concept of service, such as waiting on tables, is derived from the Greek word for <u>ministry.</u> God wants Christians to accept the privilege of serving unbelievers by proclaiming a desire to be reconciled.

We must get with them in an environment where they can talk freely. The most important thing in Building Close Relationships is the one-on-one or two-on-two activities.

The best style here is the serving style. We should serve them in ways that will get their attention. Use your time and financial resources and watch God work.

Building Casual Spiritual Relationships

- Start spiritual conversations
  - Question / bridge
- Start an Evangelical prayer list
- Invite them to church related activities
- Give them books to read
- Use an Invitational Style

At this stage we must make the jump to having spiritual conversations. Have a spiritual conversation starter question ready and use it, such as "Are you a church goer?" Also, be ready to bridge from a natural conversation, and this bridge is best when made in the form of a question. An example would be that you are on a walking trail with your neighbor and you are discussing the beauty in nature. A good bridge question would be, "Did you ever wonder how all this came about?"

Also now you should have an evangelical prayer list that you pray over daily, and be inviting. Ask them to church related activities: socials first then church services later. Then the best style from *Becoming a Contagious Christian* is the Invitational Style.

Building Close Spiritual Relationships

- Learn some basic apologetics
- Start a relational seeker small group
- Use an Intellectual Style

Now you have had some spiritual conversations, and they are asking harder questions. You need to go deeper, and if you don't know the answers you should get help or just find out yourself. At least learn some basic apologetics to the most common questions. Since you are engaging in good spiritual dialogue, the best style at this point is the Intellectual Style. It's important not to be defensive or argumentative; just do the research and get back to them later. Remember "I don't know" is still a good answer but don't leave them hanging.

Building Deep Spiritual Relationships

- Challenge them to seek God
- Keep spiritual conversations ongoing

- Take them to a basic class in Christianity
- Start an evangelistic Bible study
- Use a Direct Style

At this point you are having some deep spiritual conversations, but they still have not crossed the line of faith. God is clearly at work in their hearts, and they need to seek Him on their own. Remember Jamie's superman story and just challenge them to seek God or simply ask them to listen to the voice of God, and He will direct you.

Keep spiritual conversations on going, and if possible invite them to a basic class in Christianity at your church. If you can, start an evangelical Bible study in your community. If you can't lead it, perhaps you can be the host and do the inviting, and a friend or pastor of your church could lead it. Now you can be very direct in your conversations and the appropriate evangelistic style is the Direct Style.

Bringing Them into the Family of God

- Tell your story
- Give a gospel presentation

You have been patient and have invested much of your life into them; God has worked, and they are ready. They just need a little more help. Telling your conversion story and walking them through a gospel presentation could be that help. As you rejoice in the new found relationship your friend has with God, remember even the angels in heaven are rejoicing. You are now no longer separated but brothers or sisters in Christ.

You are now ready to step out, but what is that next step?

Small group discussion or personal reflection questions

1. Which evangelistic style fits you best?

   • Interpersonal, serving, invitational, intellectual, direct

2. With which evangelistic style do you need to get help?

3. What is a new way in which you can serve unbelievers?

Chapter 15

Now What?

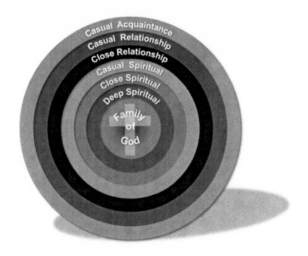

*I*f after reading this book you still are not excited about reaching people for Christ maybe your own faith is weak. Do you really believe that those outside of Christ are destined to spend eternity in hell? One survey states that 57% of evangelical Christians in America believe that many religions can lead to eternal life. If you fall into that category then please spend some time strengthening your faith. Romans 10:17 states that "faith comes from hearing and hearing by the word of Christ." You need to be listening to God, and the best way to do that is by reading, studying, and meditating on His word, the Bible. So get involved in a Bible study group, do your own personal study, and get plugged into a good Bible teaching church. Jesus said in John 14:6, "I am the way, and the truth, and the life, no one comes to the Father but through Me." Christ is the only way, and we must sincerely believe that before we can influence others to believe it.

But if you have read the book and you have caught the vision of building relationships, you now see that evangelism is not only the giving of the gospel but getting people to the point at which they will receive it gladly. George Barna says, "Just as our nation's culture has changed over the last 30 years, so has the way in which people come to Christ. The weekend church service is no longer the primary mechanism for salvation decisions; only one out of every ten believers who makes a decision to follow Christ does so in a church setting or service. On the other hand, personal relationships have become even more important in evangelism, with a majority of salvation decisions coming in direct response to an invitation by a family member or friend."

Take a minute and prayerfully evaluate where you are in that process. Do you need to get plugged into or start a non-church activity? Or maybe you should move to more one-on-one activities and focus on starting spiritual conversations. Maybe you are ready to start a seeker small group or an evangelistic Bible study. Or just maybe all of the above are true, and you are eager to go. So plan your next step or steps and just do it!

As you move forward, two areas of concern that I would like to give you. The first is that of making sure that the relationships that you are building are not romantic relationships. For the relationships with the opposite sex, get help from your spouse or a mixed group of friends. Second, when you invite people into your home never surprise them with an invitation to donate to a special cause or to purchase something. Nothing will damage the relationship that you are building more than by communicating to them that you want their money, no matter how good the cause.

Also remember that not everything succeeds. If you try an activity or if you start a relationship and it isn't successful, do not be discouraged but just move to other activities and start other relationships without giving up on the ones you have. Be patient and get help and encouragement from other Christians. Galatians 6:9, "Let us not lose heart in doing good, for in due time we will reap if we do not grow weary." So stay connected to a Christian small group or church community group so they can lift you up in times of discouragement. We need each other especially in the area of evangelism.

II Timothy 4:5, "But you, be sober in all things, endure hardship, do the work of an evangelist, fulfill your ministry." Finally, you cannot imagine what God can accomplish through you if you are willing. So fulfill the work that God has called you to do.

Do the work of a **RELATIONAL EVANGELIST** and

Keep Looking Up,
   Ron

Small group discussion or personal reflection questions

1. What about the book was most revealing to you?

2. What about the book was most challenging?

3. What does God want you to do?

- This week

- This month

- This year

Possible Small Group Format – 2 hours

- Opening prayer and snacks – 15min
- First reading – 15min
- First discussion – 30min
- Second reading – 15min
- Second discussion – 30min
- Prayer requests and closing prayer – 15min

Seven week small group outline:

Week 1

- First Reading -Introduction and Chapter 1, Discuss questions at the end of chapter 1
- Second Reading – Chapter 2, Discuss questions at the end of chapter 2

Week 2

- First Reading -Chapter 3, Discuss questions at the end of chapter 3
- Second Reading – Chapter 4, Discuss questions at the end of chapter 4

Week 3

- First Reading -Chapter 5, Discuss questions at the end of chapter 5
- Second Reading – Chapter 6, Discuss questions at the end of chapter 6

Week 4

- First Reading -Chapter 7, Discuss questions at the end of chapter 7
- Second Reading – Chapter 8, Discuss questions at the end of chapter 8

Week 5

- First Reading -Chapter 9, Discuss questions at the end of chapter 9
- Second Reading – Chapter 10, Discuss questions at the end of chapter 10

Week 6

- First Reading -Chapter 11, Discuss questions at the end of chapter 11
- Second Reading – Chapter 12, Discuss questions at the end of chapter 12

Week 7

- First Reading -Chapter 13, Discuss questions at the end of chapter 13
- Second Reading – Chapters 14 and 15, Discuss questions at the end of chapters 14 & 15

Bibliography

Aldrich, Joseph C. *Life-style Evangelism: Crossing Traditional Boundaries to Reach the Unbelieving World*. Portland, OR: Multnomah, 1981. Print.

"The Barna Group - 20 Years of Surveys Show Key Differences in the Faith of America's Men and Women." *The Barna Group - 20 Years of Surveys Show Key Differences in the Faith of America's Men and Women*. N.p., n.d. Web. 13 July 2012.

"The Barna Group - A New Generation Expresses Its Skepticism and Frustration with Christianity." *The Barna Group - A New Generation Expresses Its Skepticism and Frustration with Christianity*. N.p., n.d. Web. 18 May 2012.

"The Barna Group - Americans Identify Their Most Important Relationships." *The Barna Group – Americans Identify Their Most Important Relationships*. N.p., n.d. Web. 20 Dec. 2011.

"The Barna Group - Evangelism Is Most Effective Among Kids." *The Barna Group - Evangelism Is Most Effective Among Kids*. N.p., n.d. Web. 12 Mar. 2012.

"The Family under Attack." *Legatus Magazine RSS*. N.p., n.d. Web. 28 Jan. 2013.

Hybels, Bill, and Mark Mittelberg. *Becoming a Contagious Christian*. Grand Rapids, MI: Zondervan Pub. House, 1994. Print.

Hybels, Bill. *Just Walk across the Room: Simple Steps Pointing People to Faith*. Grand Rapids, MI: Zondervan, 2006. Print.

Jeremiah, David. *Signs of Life*. Nashville, TN: Thomas Nelson, 2007. Print.

"John MacArthur Study Bible." *John MacArthur Study Bible*. N.p., n.d. Web. 28 Jan. 2013.

"The Last Days." *The Decline Of Christianity In America*. N.p., n.d. Web. 12 Mar. 2012.

Lucado, Max, and David Drury. *Out Live Your Life: Participant's Guide*. Nashville, TN: Thomas Nelson, 2010. Print.

Mittelberg, Mark, Lee Strobel, and Bill Hybels. *Becoming a Contagious Christian: Communicating Your Faith in a Style That Fits You: Participant's Guide*. Grand Rapids, MI: Zondervan Pub. House, 1995. Print.

Poole, Garry. *Seeker Small Groups: Engaging Spiritual Seekers in Life-changing Discussions*. Grand Rapids, MI: Zondervan, 2003. Print.

Richardson, Don. *Peace Child*. Glendale, CA: G/L Regal, 1974. Print.

Solomon, Lon. *The 23rd Psalm for the 21st Century: A Jewish Shepherd's Story*. San Francisco, CA: Purple Pomegranate Productions, 2008. Print.

"Statistics and Research Provided by LifeWay Research." *National Back to Church Sunday*. N.p., n.d. Web. 18 May 2012.

Strobel, Lee. *The Case for Faith: A Journalist Investigates the Toughest Objections to Christianity*. Grand Rapids, MI: ZondervanPublishingHouse, 2000. Print.

Swindoll, Charles R. *Come before Winter: . . . and Share My Hope*. Porthant: Multnomah, 1985. Print.

Van Biema, David. "Christians: No One Path to Salvation."
    Time. N.p., 23 June 2008. Web. 26
    Jan. 2013. <http://www.time.com/time>.

Acknowledgments

I am grateful to all who have guided, participated, encouraged, and prayed for the completion of this book. The process was far more than I had anticipated, and it started with my good friend Jamie Jackson's asking me to teach about evangelism to our senior adult community group at McLean Bible Church. I had never viewed myself as an evangelist, just like most everyone else who will read this book, but Jamie saw what was happening in our community and wanted others to benefit from it. So, that was the beginning.

I am grateful to our McLean Bible Church small group who prayed for me and encouraged me along the way. Also I would thank them for being the first to read and discuss it based on the small group format. A special thanks goes to group member Paul Montgomery who redesigned my Relational Evangelism graphic.

Thank you to those who wrote articles for the book: Jamie Winship, Monica Ross, Marissa Cowell, and Lon Solomon from his book.

I would also like to thank the readers who gave me helpful critiques: Larry Gray, Pete Rockx, and my son Ryan. I thank the Tuesday night Bible study group: Jamie, Patrick, Don, Jack, Steve, and Jerry, for their support in this endeavor.

A special thank you to my wife Carol for her support and to my daughter Renee Peterson. Renee put in long hours correcting and editing my feeble attempt at English. She also made some good suggestions such as adding the questions at the end of each chapter.

Finally, I am truly grateful to my Lord and Savior Jesus Christ, for saving me and allowing me to serve Him in this way. God is truly at work, and I am living a dream.

CPSIA information can be obtained at www.ICGtesting.com
Printed in the USA
BVOW031606050413

317436BV00002B/2/P